SPHE: 3rd Year

Minding Me 3
My Well-Being

Includes the SIX official Well-Being indicators

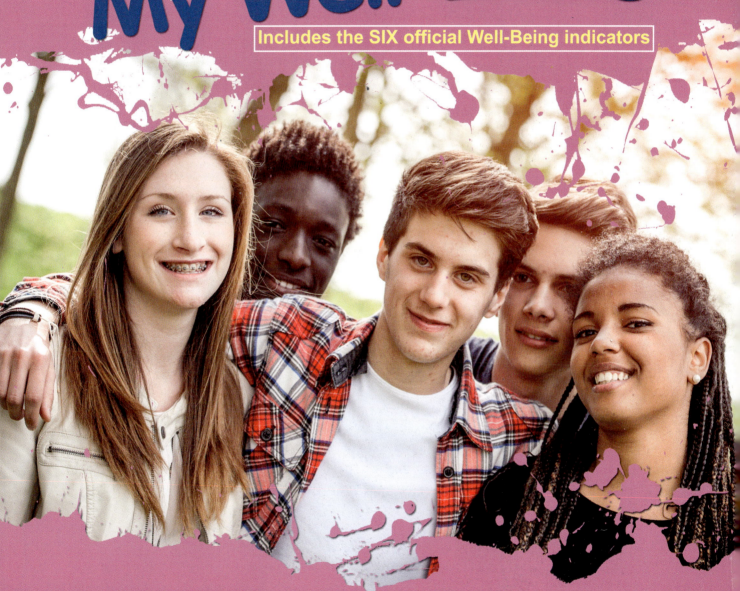

Social, Personal and Health Education

Fiona Chambers   Anne Jones   Anita Stackpoole

MENTOR

MENTOR BOOKS
43 Furze Road
Sandyford Industrial Estate
Dublin 18
Tel: 01-2952112
Fax: 01-2952114
Website: www.mentorbooks. ie
Email: admin@mentorbooks. ie

Text:	Fiona Chambers
	Anne Jones
	Anita Stackpoole
Subject editor:	Joan Rath
Edited by:	Emma Dunne
Artwork:	QBS Learning
Design and layout:	Kathryn O'Sullivan
Cover Design:	Kathryn O'Sullivan

Acknowledgements

The publisher would like to thank the following for permission to reproduce material: Rory O'Neill, Henry Holt & Company, Faber & Faber.

The publisher has made every effort to trace and acknowledge the holders of copyright for material in this book. In the event of any copyright holder having been overlooked, the publishers will come to a suitable arrangement at the first opportunity.

ISBN: 978-1-909417-67-0

Contents

Introduction

In the *Minding Me: My Well-Being* series, we want to create a space for you to stop and think about your well-being. You will learn about the steps you can take to ensure that you are happy, healthy and well. There are 8 key skills to help you feel your best and ready for life's challenges:

- being creative
- being literate (i.e. able to read, write and spell at the right level for your age-group)
- being numerate (i.e. able to understand mathematical reasoning and problem solve at the right level for your age-group)
- communicating
- managing information and thinking
- managing yourself
- staying well
- working with others

In this book, you will complete a number of activities that we have carefully designed to help you to develop these core life skills.

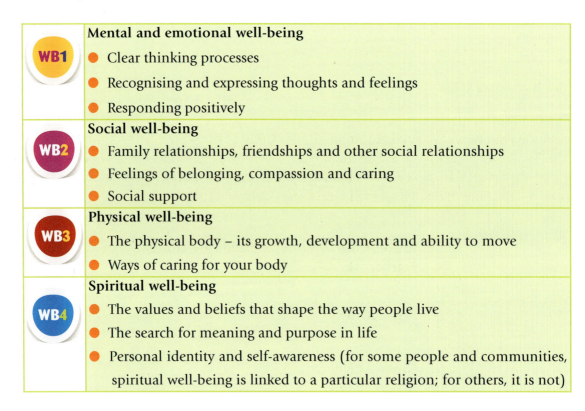

While moving through this book, the icons above will be helpful in identifying which type of well-being is being explored. All four types of well-being work together to ensure an overall sense of well-being.

We have also included the six official Well-being indicators. These six indicators appear regularly throughout the series:

The icons below are used to show you how SPHE links to other topics and skills.

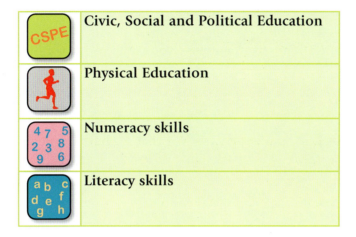

CSPE	**Civic, Social and Political Education**
	Physical Education
	Numeracy skills
	Literacy skills

As this is your third and final year in the Junior Cycle of the school, you will find that a lot of the activities in this book are discussions aimed at helping you make informed decisions about important life choices. This book will provide a strong foundation for you as you move to a senior cycle SPHE & Well-Being programme next year.

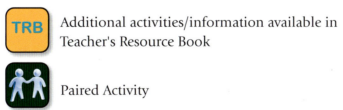

TRB	Additional activities/information available in Teacher's Resource Book
	Paired Activity
	Group Activity

Fiona, Anne and Anita

Module 1
Belonging and Integrating

Welcome back to school – or perhaps to your new school. In this module we will look at how to approach your Third Year in secondary school. We will encourage you to take control of your own destiny and enhance your experience of school life and your personal well-being.

 Digital Resources are available for this module at mentorbooks.ie/resources

We will explore:

1. Looking back, looking forward

It's good to start Third Year in secondary school on a positive note. That positive note is identifying whom you have become over the years and where this can lead you. You may have learned a great deal over the summer months from new experiences which could give more direction to your life.

1 Changes

To help you realise how you have grown and explore your expectations for Third Year, answer the questions below. Keep your answers simple – words rather than sentences.

(a) What new responsibilities have you taken on since last year (e.g. part-time work, volunteering, minding younger brothers/sisters/cousins)?

_____

(b) How do you think these new responsibilities have added to your character?

_____

(c) What activities, if any, did you take part in during your summer holidays?

_____

(d) What motivated you to participate in these activities?

_____

(e) Can you describe how you have changed as a person since last year?

_____

Try to keep hold of the positive feelings you experienced during the summer by repeating some of the activities you enjoyed over the break, such as hiking with friends, trying different foods, reading a good book etc. And remember it's never too late to take up a new activity – now might be just the time to start. Nurture the new you!

NOTE
Take a little time to yourself and recall a really nice scene from your holidays. Think about it as a quick relaxation exercise.

New start, new school year: let's get motivated!

There is a reason why people do things: it is called motivation, the drive to get up and go, but it takes many forms.

ACTIVITY

TRB

2 **What motivates you?**

One motivation is the desire to achieve your best in an activity. List two other things below that you think could motivate people to take action.

(a)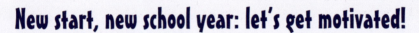

(b)

WB1

Motivations can be divided into two categories.

1. **Intrinsic** (think of the word *internal*: how we feel on the inside) – when people do something for the joy of doing it (a hobby) or because they believe it is the right thing to do.

Martin Luther King Jr (1929–1968) was an American Baptist minister, activist, humanitarian and leader in the African American Civil Rights Movement.

Emmeline Pankhurst (1858–1928) was a leading British women's rights activist who campaigned for the right for women to vote, which was finally won in 1928.

2. **Extrinsic** (think of the word *external*: from the outside) – when people do something to get something (a medal, an award or a payment).

Getting paid is an extrinsic motivation.

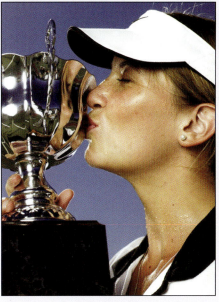

The opportunity to win awards can drive people to achieve their best.

ACTIVITY

3 My motivations

(a) Write three things that motivate you on three separate small pages or Post-It notes.

(b) Review the descriptions of intrinsic and extrinsic on page 9. Do you think your motivations are mostly intrinsic or extrinsic?

_____

(c) Have a show of hands in the class and count how many people are mostly extrinsically motivated and how many are mostly intrinsically motivated.

(d) Discuss as a class:

(i) What are people in the class most motivated by, intrinsic or extrinsic factors?

(ii) If you were a group leader, how could you use this information to motivate your class group?

4 Analysis

Looking at the results of the previous activity, answer the following questions.

(a) Suggest three ways you might improve the motivation of your class group to work towards your academic goals.

(i) _____

(ii) _____

(iii) _____

(b) How do you think your personal levels of motivation might affect your future?

_____

❝The will to win, the desire to succeed, the urge to reach your full potential … these are the keys that will unlock the door to personal excellence.❞

Confucius

USER:
STUDENT

PASSWORD:
MOTIVATION

2. Goal-setting for Third Year

Paired ACTIVITY

1 **Sayings**

With your partner, discuss the sayings below. How do you think they might be relevant to your Third Year in school?

'Strike while the iron is hot.'

'Make hay while the sun shines.'

The sayings above suggest taking action, recognising opportunities and making the best of a situation. Deciding **now** how you want to approach this challenging year is the best approach. Taking charge and responsibility from the outset will give you a better chance of success. Succeeding in your goals will create a great sense of energy, accomplishment and happiness. This will greatly enhance your feelings of well-being.

Whatever you can do, or dream you can, be it now. Boldness has genius, power and magic in it. Begin it now!

Goethe

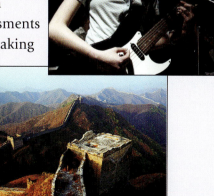

Getting your Junior Cycle Profile of Achievement is the big challenge of Third Year, but it need not be the only focus in your life. Events in your personal life can enhance your performance at exams and in assessments as they will demonstrate that you are capable of taking on challenges. It is also important to remember that other activities will see you through stressful times ahead. Goals for the future – such as finding it easier to make friends, not being afraid of speaking in public, improving your guitar-playing skills, learning to cope with and ignore peer pressure and even deciding to travel the world – involve planning and can be worked on in Third Year.

ACTIVITY

2 **Goals**

(a)   List your personal goals for Third Year.

_____

_____

_____

WB1

(b)   Where would you like to see yourself in five years' time?

_____

_____

_____

(c)   List the goals you need to achieve in order to get there.

_____

_____

_____

3 **My five-year plan**

Use the goals you identified in the previous activity to draw up your five-year plan. To do this you need to 'plan backwards to implement forwards' and identify all the mini-goals you need to achieve to reach your ultimate goal. Have a look at the example of Laura's plan below to give you an idea of how to proceed.

Short-term goals	Medium-term goals	Long-term goals
By the end of this term I will . . .	**In one year's time I will . . .**	**In five years' time I will . . .**
Have a suitable study plan in place for weekdays and weekends.	Have a Junior Cycle Profile of Achievement containing good grades in my exam subjects and positive feedback in my assessment tasks.	Be in my second year of nursing training.
Be spending an extra half-hour on Maths three times a week.	Have got summer work in the local nursing home.	Be renting a house with my friends.
Have set up a study group for Science and History.		Go to America to work for my summer holidays.
Be training in basketball two nights a week.		
Have looked up nursing colleges on the web and checked exactly what points I need to get into college.		

12

Remember to follow the steps below when working out your five-year plan:

Step One: Write in your long-term goals

Step Two: Write in your medium-term goals

Step Three: Write in your short-term goals

MY FIVE-YEAR PLAN		
Long-term goals	**Medium-term goals**	**Short-term goals**
In five years' time I will . . .	**In one year's time I will . . .**	**By the end of this term I will . . .**

Make sure you review your plan regularly and tick off the goals you have achieved. If you find you are not achieving the goals you have set:

(i) Ask yourself why this has happened.

(ii) If the goal was unrealistic, you need to reset the goal to make it more achievable.

4 **Characteristics**

Being able to work towards a goal shows characteristics that are important in today's competitive world. What do you think some of those characteristics are?

(a) _____

(b) _____

(c) _____

3. Work contract

1 **Contract**

If everyone in the class is to achieve their absolute best in the Junior Cycle Profile of Achievement, the whole class needs to set some rules to create a good learning environment. To do this, it will be necessary to draw up a work contract for you and your class group. Look at the sample work contract below to help you make up your personal work contract.

Personal Work Contract

I, _____, promise to:

1. Listen in class

2. Respect other pupils by

    _____

3. Respect teachers by

    _____

Signed: _____

Date: _____

2 **Ensuring learning**

(a) In small groups, decide on three ways that you can ensure that your class learns.

(i) _____

(ii) _____

(iii) _____

WB1

WB2

(b)   Appoint a spokesperson to feed your group's ideas back to your teacher.

(c)   Then decide as a class on the top ten factors.

(d)   Include the top ten factors your class has chosen in the group work contract below:

Group Work Contract

As a group, we, class _____, want to have a positive learning atmosphere in all our classes. To do this we will:

1.   _____

2.   _____

3.   _____

4.   _____

5.   _____

6.   _____

7.   _____

8.   _____

9.   _____

10. _____

What you get by achieving your goals is not as important as what you become by achieving your goals.

Zig Ziglar, American author and motivational speaker

End of Module Review

WB4

Design a poster to inspire young people to pursue a personal goal. It must include a motivational slogan. Perhaps display the posters around the Year 3 and Year 6 areas to encourage and support fellow students in your school.

 Remember!

An effective poster should be visually pleasing, clear and attract the viewer's attention.

Module 2
Self-Management

This module focuses on achieving goals, time management and coping skills for examinations.

 Digital Resources are available for this module at mentorbooks.ie/resources

We will explore:

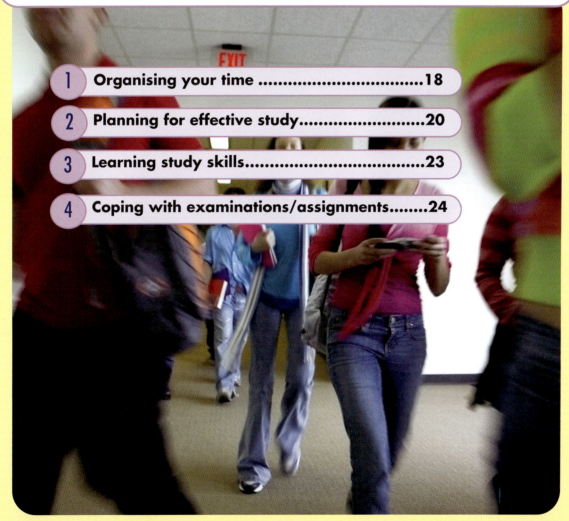

1. Organising your time

'Tempus Fugit' – time flies ...

It is important to organise your time so that you can spend it effectively.

1 **How balanced is your life?**

(a) In the timetable below, fill in how much time you spend each day at the activities listed. Then total the time spent each week on each activity.

	Mon	Tues	Wed	Thurs	Fri	Sat	Sun	Total
School								
Homework/study								
After-school activities								
Radio/TV/music								
Social media								
Gaming								
Sport								
Phone								
Meeting friends								
Eating								
Sleeping								
Other								

(b)   Look at how you filled out your table. Identify three areas you think you would like to change and why.

(i)   _____

(ii) _____

(iii) _____

(c)   How might it benefit you to spend less time watching TV or gaming etc.?

_____

_____

(d)   What would you like to do with this extra time in your day?

_____

_____

2   Screen time

As a class group, add up the time spent looking and working at screens.

(a)   Discuss the benefits of screen time.

(b)   Discuss the drawbacks of screen time.

(c)   Draw up a class agreement on screen time, stating how much time per week you think is appropriate and agreeing to stick to it for a week.

Remember!

There are 24 hours in the day. You spend 8 hours sleeping, 2 hours eating, 7 hours at school and 2–3 hours on homework. That leaves about 4 hours for other activities! Choose well … Getting the best from your day is all about organising your time.

2. Planning for effective study

You are now approaching a time in your school life where you may have more assignments, deadlines or exams, so it is important to have an effective study plan as this will allow you to find the time in your day to do the other things that you want. Studying can be seen as a strategy towards self-improvement. It can certainly strengthen your chances in an exam situation as well as pave the way for future learning.

Prepare your materials

- In every class take careful notes. Review all notes at least once a week (for more difficult classes you should do this every day). Keep your notes in an organised notebook and do additional research on material that is not clear to you. (Keep this additional information in your notebook as well.)

- Read all written materials thoroughly and take notes or highlight all important facts or concepts.
- Create flashcards for more difficult concepts or facts; hang them on your bedroom wall and review them daily. Discuss questions and problem areas with your teacher on a regular basis.
- Participate in class – you will remember more when you are actively involved in the class.
- Take advantage of or create study groups for more difficult classes.
- Work through every homework assignment carefully.
- When you receive the information about an assignment or an exam, start planning how you will prepare for it that first night.

Prepare your body

- Be rested, fed and fit!
- Get the right amount of sleep.
- Eat three reasonably nutritious meals a day, with plenty of fruit and vegetables.
- Reduce your intake of caffeine and sugar, and avoid fatty foods.
- Drink eight glasses of water a day and remember to bring some water into the exam centre with you.
- Exercise regularly.

Prepare your mind

Planning for effective study really depends on your attitude. By shifting your mindset from passive to positive, you stand a better chance of overcoming the fear of even starting to study. You need to find out what works best for you, so here are some guidelines to help you get started:

- Think positive. Think of the athlete who wins the race: what makes that athlete a winner is his/her positive mental attitude. How much you believe in yourself will make the difference. Apparently we talk to ourselves thousands of times a day. Try turning some of that self-chat into positive statements like 'I can do it'. That, in itself, is a good start. Positive thinking is a powerful force.

- Watch out for negative or critical self-talk before a test (or at any other time). Dispute it! Argue with it! Out-talk it!

- To help clear your mind, do a relaxation or meditation exercise daily (don't knock it until you've tried it!).

- Avoid talking about study and 'just do it!' Don't wait to be 'in the mood' and don't make excuses.

- Break your tasks up into small pieces and reward yourself after you've done each bit. Develop your goals – for the term, the year and the next five years. Make goals realistic, clear and linked to your studies. Make sure they are your goals – not Mum's, Dad's or your friends'.

- Don't forget to check your study plan regularly. Change strategies that do not work for you and keep looking for solutions to problem areas. Ask your teacher to help you.

Learning styles

Use your preferred learning style. Your learning style is the way in which you learn best. The three most common learning styles are auditory, visual and tactile/kinaesthetic. Which one are you?

- An **auditory** learner responds best to information given in an auditory language format. They enjoy listening to audiotapes, lectures and debates.

- A **visual** learner learns best when information is presented in written or picture format. Visual learners usually recall information by creating pictures in their minds.

- A **tactile/kinaesthetic** learner likes physical activities. They enjoy a more hands-on approach in their learning. They need room to move and are very good at manipulating objects.

When you know what *your* learning style is, it will make studying a lot easier for you. If you are an auditory learner perhaps record yourself talking through your notes or check out webinars that might be available online to support you. If your preferred style is visual, maybe draw images to help you remember material. If you are a kinaesthetic learner, experiments, role playing and games might work for you.

How do we remember things?

We have two types of memory and where the information is stored depends on what we are learning:

1. **Short-term memory** (STM) = this holds information for 15 seconds, if it is not transferred into long-term memory. If we repeat words/sentences over and over, it can be transferred into ...

2. **Long-term memory** (LTM) = this retains information over a longer period, e. g. hours, days, weeks, years.

Tips for learning

1. Make a connection: try to make links between new information and stored information. When you are learning, your brain needs to encode the information to store it (encoding means how information is changed so you can store it in your memory).

2. Spread out your learning time: cramming does not really work, as you will only remember the information for about an hour or two.

3. Use rhymes, acronyms and stories to help you create meaning for information.

4. Acronyms are good if you need to learn a list. Acronyms are words that are formed from the initial letters of other words, e. g. ROI is Republic of Ireland.

5. You could also try using mnemonics to help you remember list items. This is a way of creating meaningless connections (in a phrase or verse) to help retrieval of information. See the examples in Activity 1 below.

1 **Remembering lists**

Can you think of a list you need to learn? Try to make an acronym for this list to make it easier to remember. We have given you an example to start you off!

Subject 1	Science: colours of the rainbow
List	Red, Orange, Yellow, Green, Blue, Indigo, Violet
Acronym	ROYGBIV
Mnemonic	Richard of York Gave Battle in Vain
Subject 2	
List	
Acronym	
Mnemonic	

3. Learning study skills

Developing study skills means building good habits. Here are some suggestions:

- Read the information first – a couple of times if necessary.
- Divide the information into smaller sections.
- Read the smaller sections to check you understand what is being said.
- Write the information in your own words or in point form.
- Learn the smaller paragraphs one at a time.
- Recall the information by testing yourself.
- Maybe write a question or two for each section you are learning.
- Remember key words to help you recall information.

 Remember!

Your 'one good adult' is the person you can turn to in a time of need – someone you can trust and rely on to advise and help you.

① **One good adult**

Sean is really worried about school at the moment. He has three assignments due this week and he hasn't even started them. He sends a text to his older brother, Paulie, who is in college in Dublin. He sees him as his one good adult and knows he can tell him anything. Read Sean's text and then, on the blank screen, write what you think Paulie's response would be (include emojis if you like).

Hi Paulie, things not good here, 3 assignments due this week, nothing done, don't know what to do … haven't told Mam yet …

4. Coping with assignments/examinations

From the beginning of Third Year, it's really important that you are familiar with your assignment due dates and your exam timetable.

ACTIVITY

1 **Assignments**

Fill in your assignment deadlines in the table below.

Date/month	Subject	Time required	Format	Planned date of completion

2 **Exam subjects**

(a) Find out each exam subject's requirements and write them into the table below.

Subject	Time per paper	Number of papers	Number of sections	Do I have a choice?

(b) In your copybook, you might like to make out a time plan for your revision for Christmas exams and later exams or assignments.

Remember!

Be careful not to misread the exam timetable or the question being asked. Practise reading the timetable and study how exam questions are worded in your exam papers.

How to relax

Relax: to make or become less tense or anxious.

Oxford English Dictionary, 2003

During Third Year, it is important that you take time to **relax**. Take some time away from your studies to enjoy your hobbies, listen to music, read, exercise or spend time with friends. Many students become anxious and worry that they won't get all of their study done. By planning and organising, you can achieve everything you need to achieve, but remember to relax.

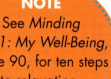

NOTE
See *Minding Me 1: My Well-Being*, page 90, for ten steps to relaxation.

Paired ACTIVITY

3 **Relaxation**

With your partner, discuss the following.

(a) How important is it to relax?

(b) Can you think of some ways to help you relax? Write your suggestions in the table below.

	Mon	Tues	Wed	Thurs	Fri	Sat	Sun	Total
Time relaxing								
Way of relaxing								

Remember!

Relax – if you are stressed or anxious about an exam, it might cause you to go blank.

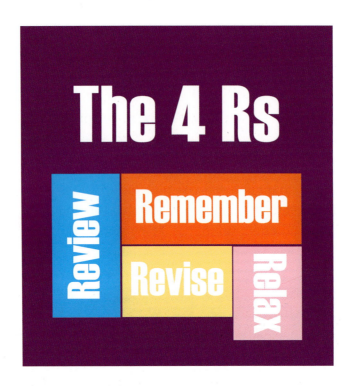

End of Module Review

It can be difficult to stay positive when you have so much to do, so remember to focus on what you are already doing well.

Look at the examples in the table below and then fill in what you are already doing to help prepare for your exams and assessment tasks and what you might like to try, remembering what you have already learned in this module.

Things that I'm doing	Things I would like to try
• Using a study plan • Drinking more water	• Use flashcards for important facts • Do a relaxation exercise each night before studying

Module 3
Communication Skills

This module will help you to build effective communication skills for all situations. Learning to communicate in a positive way with those around us is an important skill for a happy and healthy life.

 Digital Resources are available for this module at mentorbooks.ie/resources

We will explore:

1. Learning to communicate

It is important to understand how improving our communication skills can enhance our relationships in our school, home and personal lives. Reaching an understanding in a situation of conflict involves sensitive discussion and active listening. Encouraging the use of honest and open discussion helps reduce the risk of offending others or of conflict.

Communication skills of good communicators

Believe it or not, the best communicators are very good at listening as well as speaking. They use a technique called **active listening**. This is important for effective communication, as it is crucial for hearing and being heard. There are seven key features of active listening:

1. **Pay attention:** listen carefully to what the other person is saying.
2. **Do not judge:** no matter how sensitive or difficult the message, try hard not to judge the other person.
3. **Repeat in fewer words**: if you've listened attentively, you will understand the message and be able to repeat the other person's message in fewer words.
4. **Question:** asking questions will help the other person think more carefully about the meaning of their message.
5. **Encourage:** try to encourage the other person by using positive language.
6. **Empathise:** try to feel what the other person is feeling.
7. **Share:** sharing a personal story similar to the other person's could help form a bond with them.

To open doors...

Communication

is the key!

1 — Identifying good communication skills

WB2

Read the following dialogue. Then, with your partner, try to identify where each of the seven features of active listening are used.

MARY: My mum is very sick at the moment.

JOHN: That's awful. What's wrong with her? You don't have to tell me if you don't want to.

MARY: She gets very bad migraines.

JOHN: Migraines are supposed to be really horrible. She must have to go to bed when she gets one. How are you feeling about it? You must have to help a lot at home?

MARY: I'm really worried about her, and it's made things pretty tough at home. I have to cook dinners and all the rest.

JOHN: I bet you're doing a brilliant job, but can I do anything to help? You must be feeling pretty bad too. My mum used to suffer from back pain and have to stay in bed a lot when I was in First Year, so I understand how it feels.

2 — Invent a conversation

Can you write a conversation that shows the seven features of active listening? Using the numbers in the **Communication skills of Good Communicators** list on the previous page, tag where each skill is used in the sentences.

_____

_____

_____

_____

_____

_____

_____

_____

Remember!

In order to develop these skills, you will need to practise them. Perhaps put the seven key words into your phone to remind you to use them.

2. Communication in situations of conflict

Conflict is . . .

A serious disagreement or argument that often involves a lot of negotiation to resolve or to find a solution agreeable to all parties involved.

Conflict can arise when two or more people view a particular situation differently. It is important in these situations to try to reach an understanding. Depending on the evidence, you may decide to change or not to change your view. But it is very important to listen to and consider the views of the opposing side.

Below are some of the ways in which conflict can be created. We call these **communication roadblocks**. They can stop communication immediately. Learning to avoid these can ensure that your message and the messages of others are heard and understood.

1 Communication roadblocks

Select five of the communication roadblocks listed on the previous page. Write each roadblock on one of the signs below. Beside each sign, write a sentence that represents the roadblock.

Interrupting

'Yeah, yeah, I know – wait till I tell you my news!'

_____

_____

_____

_____

_____

2 Communication roadblocks in the classroom

In small groups, identify the communication roadblock you find most annoying in the classroom. Each group should state its chosen roadblock to the class. When all groups have given their chosen roadblock, work out which one got the most votes. How can you work as a class to remove this roadblock?

NOTE
Some people listen to understand and others listen to respond.

Removing communication roadblocks

Using the I-message can be a really good strategy to remove communication roadblocks. It places you, your feelings and what you want at the centre of the message. Your feelings are how *you* feel and cannot be disputed by the other person. Feelings are fact.

The I-message or I-statement

The **I-message** (I-statement) was developed by Thomas Gordon in the 1960s to help people become more assertive. By using an I-message, you can tell a person how their behaviour makes you feel and how you might wish their behaviour to change in the future in a strong and positive way. There are three parts to the I-message:

1. **I feel** (state the feeling)
2. **When you** (state the other person's behaviour)
3. **I want** (state what you want to happen in future)

Example:

'I felt really hurt when you didn't invite me to go to the cinema with you last weekend because we're friends. I would like to be included in future.'

ACTIVITY

3 **Using the I-message**

Dear _____ (your one good adult),

Most days at school my friend Rhona asks me for lunch money, saying she forgot to get it from her mum. She never pays me back. I need to talk to her about this because I am very angry with her.

Bridget

What should Bridget say to Rhona? Write your answer as an I-statement from Bridget.

_____

_____

Inner conflict

Inner or internal conflict can be defined as a state of confusion or struggle within the mind as a result of the messages we communicate to ourselves on a daily basis. Sometimes this is a battle between doing what you think you *should* do or are *expected* to do and being your true self. It could be knowing that you're allowing a situation that you are uncomfortable with to continue. Or it could be a risk that you are trying to talk yourself into taking.

4 **Your inner conflicts**

Think of any issues in your life that are causing you inner conflict at the moment and record them on the signpost below.

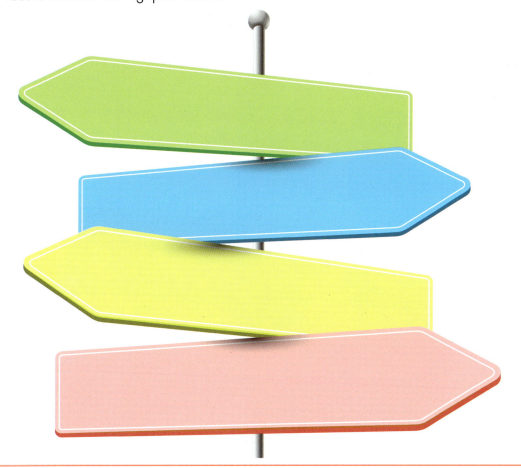

Even just making yourself aware of your inner conflicts can start to dispel them. Ignoring them or trying to distract yourself from them will only add to your feelings of stress and discomfort. Acknowledging inner conflicts can put you in touch with your real feelings and instincts and set you on the right track to resolving them.

End of Module Review

In the boxes below, design emojis to represent the three parts of the I-message.

I feel …

when you …

I want …

Module 4
Physical Health

In *Minding Me 1: My Well-Being* and *Minding Me 2: My Well-Being*, we examined how to take care of our bodies and learned about some causes of ill-health and how to treat ourselves when we are unwell.

Here, we will build on this knowledge and explore exercise, relaxation methods and eating habits – three important elements of our overall physical well-being over which we have a lot of control. Developing good habits in these areas will lead to feeling fit and able for many of life's challenges.

 Digital Resources are available for this module at mentorbooks.ie/resources

We will explore:

It's all about balance

You need to balance what you put into your body with the energy you use. Your spiritual, mental, social, emotional, physical and nutritional needs must be managed and evaluated on a regular basis for you to remain healthy.

Throughout our lives there may be times when we neglect one or more of these needs, e. g. during exams. When this happens it has a knock-on effect on the other needs, e.g. if you don't eat healthy foods, you don't have the energy to exercise.

1. Physical exercise

Due to many technological changes, e.g. cars, online gaming and TV, daily physical exercise has become less of a reality. This is having a direct impact on the physical health of many people and resulting in an increase in obesity.

Physical exercise not only balances energy input with output, it also releases hormones (endorphins) that make us feel good. In addition, as you become more conscious of the health benefits of exercise, you are less likely to choose to eat unhealthy foods.

In Third Year, with the Junior Cycle exams approaching, many students feel they don't have the time for exercise because they need to study. It is important to remember that some exercise every day will energise you and help you to concentrate better when you are studying.

 ## Remember!

Thirty minutes of moderate-to-intense exercise every day will help keep you fit and healthy (moderate-to-intense exercise is when you are sweating and your heart is beating fast). Be sure to choose an activity that you like or enjoy – then you're more likely to keep it up. Maybe do an activity with your friends.

1 Leisure activities in your area

(a) Research three healthy activities available in your area. Fill in the details in the table below.

Activity	Address	Website	Times of training	Equipment needed	Cost per session	Instructor name

(b) When you have researched the options in your area, decide which activity you would like to do and keep a diary for a couple of weeks until exercise becomes a habit for you. Use the table on page 139 as a guide.

(c) Compare your list with your classmates' lists and compile a poster detailing all the activities available in your area.

2 Leisure activities you can do at home

List three healthy activities that you can do that do not require you to join a club.

(a) _____

(b) _____

(c) _____

2. Relaxation

- It is important to allow yourself time to relax as well as time to exercise.
- Mental relaxation is just as important as physical relaxation.
- Freeing our minds of thoughts or worries can help us achieve mental relaxation.
- Relaxation helps to de-stress the body; one of the simplest ways to relax is to be aware of your breathing.
- In times of stress our breathing is quick and short, but slowing down our breathing can reduce the tension we are feeling.
- Some students can become stressed during exams, so it is important to do your breathing exercises before the start of the exam to help you to relax.

Meditation

- Research has shown that meditation can bring about a healthy state of relaxation.
- Meditation aims to quieten the busy mind and focus the attention on the present. Worrying about past and future events can bring about stress.

Meditation can cause many different physiological changes:
- decreased heart rate
- decreased respiratory rate (i.e. slowing down your breathing)
- reduced stress hormone (plasma cortisol)
- decreased pulse rate
- increased brain activity associated with relaxation

After meditation:
- the body's reactions are faster
- creativity is greater
- understanding is deeper

The basic elements of traditional meditation are:
- a quiet place
- comfortable posture
- something to concentrate on, e.g. a word (mantra) or your breathing, and a passive attitude (i.e. not easily distracted; this is something that will become easier with practise).

Mindfulness

> *"Mindfulness means maintaining a moment-by-moment awareness of our thoughts, feelings, bodily sensations, and surrounding environment."*
>
> *'What Is Mindfulness?', greatergood. berkeley. edu*

Why bother meditating or practising mindfulness?

- Studies show that students who meditate before an exam perform better than students who do not.
- Mindfulness practice can improve concentration.
- Mindfulness reduces symptoms of anxiety, stress and depression.

Effects of mindfulness on the brain

Mindfulness = brain training. It increases grey matter in the part of the brain responsible for self-awareness and compassion. Think of the way physical exercise makes our bodies healthier. Mindfulness does the same for the brain.

TRB

1 Mindful eating

Our lives have become so busy that we often carry out everyday tasks, such as cleaning our teeth, taking a shower or making our breakfast without being fully present. You can probably think of a time when you arrived at school and had no recollection of what you saw along the way! A simple practice like mindful eating can help to train the mind to stay present and fully experience the task at hand. This exercise can be done with a raisin – or if you want to treat yourself, one square of chocolate.

Step 1: Put a raisin in your hand and then close your eyes. Take a few moments to become aware of your sense of touch. What does the raisin feel like? Could you describe its texture? Drop it from one hand to the other and feel the weight of the raisin in your hand.

Step 2: Put the raisin close to your nose and experience its smell. Could you describe it in your own words?

Step 3: Place the raisin in your mouth and roll it around your tongue, becoming aware of the initial taste in your mouth.

Step 4: Bite into the raisin and fully experience the taste. Is it similar to any other food? What words come to mind to help you describe the taste? Connect to your emotions. How is this making you feel?

Step 5: See if you can tune into the sensation to swallow as the raisin moves to the back of your throat. Swallow and relax into your chair.

Step 6: **Reflection:** What was it like to be fully present as you ate the raisin mindfully?

Now answer the following questions.

(a) How did the raisin taste?

_____

(b) If you have had raisins before, did they taste different when you ate this raisin mindfully?

_____

(c) Describe how you typically eat – quickly, slowly etc.

_____

(d) What did you learn from this exercise and how might you apply this experience to your life?

_____

_____

_____

(e) List five other activities that you might do mindfully.

(i) _____

(ii) _____

(iii) _____

(iv) _____

(v) _____

Mindfulness stops the mind from racing

WB4

When we practise mindfulness, we realise that our brain is always chattering, moving from thought to thought. Anxiety and worry come from negative thoughts. Mindfulness helps you to slow down and to recognise and label these thoughts as worries that are not based on reality. This stops the negative thoughts. In other words, you acknowledge the anxiety without getting caught up in the negative thoughts it generates.

NOW

3. Diet

We hear the word diet all the time in the media and generally it refers to weight loss or weight gain. Making people more aware of what they eat can result in healthier eating habits. However, becoming obsessive about diets can lead to distorted images of what a person 'should' look like.

NOTE
Diet refers to what you eat.

1 **Looking at what you eat**

As honestly as you can, fill out the table below for one day. Remember to include any drinks (tea, coffee, water etc). Identify foods you think are healthy choices (H) and those you think are unhealthy choices (U). You can refer to the food pyramid on page 42 for guidance.

Time	Example	Today's food	Servings of food eaten from each shelf of food pyramid (see p.42)
Breakfast	Orange juice (H) Cornflakes (H)		
Mid-morning break	Bar of chocolate (U)		
Lunch/Dinner	Ham and cheese sandwich (H) Bags of crisps (U) Can of coke (U)		
Mid-afternoon	Apple (H) Yoghurt (H)		
Dinner/Tea	Hamburger and chips (U) Milk (H)		
Other snacks	3 cookies (U)		

2 **Evaluating your diet**

(a) Fill out the evaluation sheet below in relation to the changes you feel you could make to improve your diet.

Now	Change
e. g. I eat no breakfast	Every morning I will eat a breakfast of cereal, fruit/juice and yoghurt
1.	
2.	
3.	

(b) Why do you think you should make these changes to your diet?

_____

_____

_____

Current healthy eating guidelines

● Eat a wide variety of foods, following the recommendations in the food pyramid below.

● Increase fruit and vegetable intake to at least five portions a day.

● Replace saturated fats, e.g. cakes, butter, with polyunsaturated alternatives, e. g. fish, nuts, vegetable oils.

● Increase fibre intake, e.g. brown bread, brown rice, fruit and vegetables.

● Reduce the amount of sugar in the diet, e.g. cakes, sweets.

● Reduce the salt intake in the diet, e.g. crisps and salt added during cooking.

● Water intake should be at least eight glasses a day.

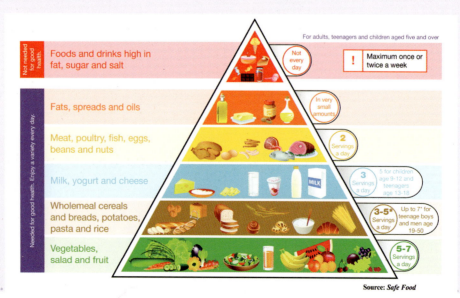

Source: *Safe Food*

42

Eat the correct quantity of food for your body size (refer to daily energy requirements in the table below).

Daily energy requirements	Male kcal	Female kcal
Children	1,500	1,400
Adolescents	2,800	2,300
Adult (sedentary, i.e. no exercise)	2,400	2,150
Adult (active)	2,800	2,450
Pregnant		2,400
Lactating		2,800
Elderly	2,200	1,800

The box below highlights foods that are high in calorie (kcal) content and foods that are low in it. Often high-kcal-content foods are also high in saturated fats.

High kcal foods		Low kcal foods	
	kcal/100g		kcal/100g
Butter	731	Banana	76
Crisps	533	Apple	46
Cheeseburger	300	Skimmed milk	33
Quarter-pounder	411	Whole milk	65
		All fruit and vegetables (majority are low cal)	

Balanced eating

Approximately one-sixth of our diet should come from protein sources; one-sixth from fats; and two-thirds from carbohydrates, including fibre. If a balanced diet is followed, vitamins and minerals will be provided in the diet.

In this module you have learned the importance of exercise, relaxation and diet. These will remain important to you throughout your life and it is important to be aware of the benefits of each.

You might find the table on page 139, at the back of the book, helpful to remind yourself about what you eat and how you relax and exercise.

End of Module Review

Write a letter to your 30-year-old self about how you looked after your physical and mental health in your teenage years.

Dear 30-year-old me . . .

Module 5

Friendship

This module explores the role of friendship in developing positive and balanced relationships, in particular with members of the opposite sex.

 Digital Resources are available for this module at mentorbooks.ie/resources

We will explore:

1. The impact of gender roles on friendships

Extensive research has been done on how children learn gender roles and opinions are divided. The following activities will help you to explore your own views.

NOTE
Gender means being male or female.

ACTIVITY

1 **Gender roles walking debate**

The classroom should be divided into three areas. One area is named Agree, one is named Disagree and one is named Unsure. When the teacher reads out each of the following statements, move to the area of the room according to whether you agree with, disagree with or are unsure about the statement.

(a) Parents tend to treat sons differently from daughters.

(b) Parents expect girls to do more housework than boys.

(c) The types of household jobs assigned to children largely depend on gender (e.g. washing dishes and laundry for girls, putting bins out and gardening for boys).

(d) Parents encourage gender stereotyping, such as girls playing with dolls and boys participating in ball games.

(e) Boys tend to be more 'rough and tumble' in their games while girls shy away from rough play.

(f) Boys have to pretend to be tougher than they are.

(g) A boy who plays almost exclusively with dolls and not typical masculine toys and who prefers to play with girls over boys is likely to be gay later in life.

(h) Romantic cross-gender (male/female) relationships generally improve a teenager's social status.

(i) Cross-gender (male/female) friendships that are not romantic are often viewed with suspicion.

2 **Walking debate review**

WB1

WB2

(a) Do you think any of the statements in Activity 1 really show how children learn gender roles?

_____

_____

_____

_____

_____

(b) Do you think any of those statements could make a person feel as if they couldn't act differently to their gender stereotype? If so, which statement in particular?

_____

(c) Ask your parents were boys and girls treated differently when they were growing up. Are there any differences between what your parents noticed and what you notice as you are growing up?

_____

_____

_____

(d) Do you think that gender stereotypes can affect a person's ability to be friends with someone of the opposite sex?

_____

_____

_____

There is nothing enlightened about shrinking so that other people won't feel insecure around you. We are all meant to shine, as children do.

Nelson Mandela in his inaugural speech, 1994

2. The benefits of having both boy-friends and girl-friends

Male

Female

ACTIVITY

1 **Discussion**

In small groups, discuss whether you think boys and girls can be just good friends.

Write down the conclusion your group reached and whether or not you agree with it.

_____

_____

_____

Platonic love and platonic friendships are relationships that are spiritual with the absence of physical or sexual attraction. If a boy and a girl spend time together regularly but aren't boyfriend and girlfriend, they'd describe their friendship as **platonic**. The word platonic refers to the writings of Plato, an ancient Greek philosopher who was the first to write on the subject of this type of friendship.

2 **Problem page**

> Dear _____ (your one good adult),
>
> Lewis and I are great friends. We have known each other since the start of First Year. It has never been an issue for us that I'm a girl and he's a boy. We just get along. Lately our friendship is being commented on by some of the girls and boys in our school. At first we didn't take the slagging to heart but now it's bothering us. We've talked about it and we both feel very uneasy now. I've noticed that we are less likely to do things together – because of how it looks and what people might say – and I miss that. What should we do?
>
> Stacey

(a) Write a response to Stacey's letter in the space below.

> Dear Stacey,
> _____
> _____
> _____
> _____
> _____
> _____

(b) Why do you think Stacey is feeling under pressure?

_____
_____

(c) Why do you think some people still find it hard to believe girls and boys can be friends?

_____
_____

WB1

WB2

Being in love

This is a phrase that we hear a lot. But what does it mean? Being in love alters you. Suddenly your life is focused on another person and you can't bear being separated from him or her. You are in a bubble of fantasy, feeling overcome and giddy.

ACTIVITY

3 Differences

(a) Why is having a boyfriend or a girlfriend different from having a boy or a girl as a friend? Fill in the table below.

Boyfriend / girlfriend	Friend

4 Balance

The following stories show two different relationships. Read the descriptions and then answer the questions.

(a) Anne and John have been going out with each other since First Year. Anne makes friends easily and likes joining in with others when she can. John has a few good friends and likes to spend time with them. Sometimes Anne and John have to plan the times they spend together so that they can also see their friends. This means that sometimes they may not see each other for a few days.

(i) Do you think this is a loving and balanced relationship?

_____

(ii) Why do you think this?

_____

_____

_____

(b) Mary and Liam have been going out for two years. They spend all their time together and even do their homework together. They have no other friends. They are always buying presents for each other.

(i) Do you think this is a loving and balanced relationship?

_____

(ii) Why do you think this?

_____

_____

Choosing a boyfriend or girlfriend

When the time comes and you feel comfortable about having a boyfriend/girlfriend, you might look for certain characteristics in the other person.

WB1

5 **Important characteristics**

What characteristics would you look for in a boyfriend or girlfriend? Place the characteristics in the list below in order of importance, with 1 being the most important to you and 12 being the least important.

Characteristic	Importance	Characteristic	Importance
Kind		Loyal	
Gentle		Respect for others	
Intelligent		Nice clothes	
Wealthy		Sense of humour	
Good-looking		Ambitious	
Sporty		Good communicator	

Can you think of three other characteristics that are important to you but which are not mentioned here?

(a) _____

(b) _____

(c) _____

6 **Class debate**

What are the differences between friendship, infatuation and love? Read the following questions and discuss them as a class.

(a) Is love the same thing as friendship?

(b) Is love simply infatuation and a biological desire to reproduce or is it more complex?

(c) Is love what we see portrayed on TV and in movies?

International Day of Friendship

In 2015 the UN secretary General Ban Ki Moon picked the International Day of Friendship, 30 July, to share this message:

'On this International Day of Friendship, let us strengthen bonds among individuals and generate greater respect and understanding in our world.'

Since its inception in 1935, Friendship Day and its celebrations have come a long way. The basic idea behind the occasion is to acknowledge your friends' contribution to your life, appreciate their presence in your life and give them your thanks.

Friendship scroll

Send a friendship scroll to a close friend. To create your friendship scroll:

- Copy the scroll template below onto coloured paper.
- At the top of the scroll neatly write the name of the friend to whom you wish to dedicate the scroll. Then finish the statement: 'You are a great friend to me because …'and list the qualities that you love most about your friend.
- Roll the paper around a pencil to make it into a scroll, remove the pencil and tie a ribbon or string around it to keep it in place.
- Present the scroll to your friend in private or hide it where you know they will find it. This would be a nice, thoughtful surprise if you notice they need a little cheering up.

Module 6
Relationships and Sexuality Education

This module examines some of the physical and emotional challenges of adolescence. We will look at ways to promote a more positive relationship with yourself and your body. Being positive about yourself will help you become more confident about choosing the people or ideas you want to be part of. We will also explore how relationships are important to our health and well-being.

 Digital Resources are available for this module at mentorbooks.ie/resources

We will explore:

1. Body image

Body image is the mental relationship you have with your body. Having a healthy body image means you feel at ease with your body.

NOTE
See also Module 7: Emotional Health.

WB1

WB3

1 **Discussion**

In groups, discuss the definition of body image given in the box above and what the phrase means to you.

The following activity should help you understand more about body image and how you feel about your own body.

Aware

2 **Personal-reflection body exercise**

This activity is best practised at home in privacy, so select a time and place where you know you will not be interrupted. Find a room with a full-length mirror, look at your body and answer these questions.

(a) Which part of my body am I looking at first – is it the part I like the most or the least?

(b) Take time to look at yourself from different angles. How does looking at yourself make you feel?

(c) Is there one area of your body that you really dislike and would like to change?

(d) Are you comparing your body to the bodies of people you have seen in the media? Do you wish you looked more like them or do you feel good as you are?

(e) If you feel a strong reaction when doing this exercise, write down your feelings in a private diary.

If you found that exercise easy and enjoyable, that is good: it means you have a positive relationship with your body.

If you found that exercise uncomfortable, it may be a good idea to look at why you found it difficult. Are you unhappy about one area of your body, e. g. nose, thighs, complexion etc.? There may be several reasons why and it is very important that you get a clear understanding of them.

If you find that you spend a lot of time thinking about the part of your body that you are dissatisfied with, then you may have an unhealthy relationship with your body. If this is not acknowledged and treated it could lead to serious health problems such as Body Dysmorphic Disorder (BDD).

Having a negative view of your body can make you worry and think about it too much. In turn, this worry can make you feel more stressed. If you feel this way, it's a good idea to talk to a friendly GP, health professional (e.g. district nurse) or a counsellor. They can help you find a way to treat these worries by talking about the reason why you may feel this way. The good news is BDD is a treatable condition.

> *Body dysmorphic disorder (BDD) is a condition that involves obsessions, which are distressing thoughts that repeatedly intrude into a person's awareness. With BDD, the distressing thoughts are about perceived appearance flaws.*
>
> *Kidshealth. org*

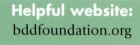

Helpful website:
bddfoundation.org

Understanding BDD

3 **Problematic areas**

(a) Complete the list of the parts of the body that you think most people would describe as problematic. Three are listed to start you off.

(i) Skin complexion, including acne and wrinkles

(ii) Height

(iii) Legs – thighs and calves

(iv) _____

(v) _____

(vi) _____

(vii) _____

(b) Joe is concerned that his calves are not as big as his teammates' on the rugby team. If Joe had BDD, how do you think he might react to this perceived flaw?

_____

_____

_____

How does BDD develop?

The exact cause of BDD is not known. However several factors can increase the likelihood of someone developing the problem, such as the natural physical changes during adolescence, experiencing negative comments, bullying or teasing and social pressures from the media.

NOTE
According to Irishhealth.com, BDD is estimated to affect 1 in every 100 people.

Talking about BDD

Hayden Panettiere

Hayden Panettiere, a well-known American actress, model, singer and activist (notable for her roles in *Nashville* and *Heroes*), openly talks about her BDD. She says her troubles began after a magazine published a picture of her aged 16 with the word 'cellulite' printed across her legs.

'I was mortified. It gave me such body dysmorphia for so long, but I remember reminding myself that beauty is an opinion, not a fact, and it has always made me feel better.

'Eating healthy is a constant battle,' Panettiere admits. 'I find when I'm overly concerned about what I eat, I stress out my body and put on weight. People can tell when you're happy with being yourself and when you're not. It's only cheesy because it's true.

'As I've gotten older and grown into my body, I've started realising that the way you carry yourself and that light coming out of your eyes are the most attractive things about you.'

Robert Pattinson

Actor Robert Pattinson (known for his roles in *Twilight* and *Harry Potter*) also revealed that he has BDD.

'I get a ton of anxiety, right up until the second I get out of the car to the [red carpet] event, when suddenly it completely dissipates. But up until that moment I'm a nut case. Body dysmorphia, overall tremendous anxiety.'

Although Pattinson is a successful movie star, he claims he frequently suffers from low self-esteem. 'I don't have a six pack and I hate going to the gym. I've been like that my whole life. I never want to take my shirt off.'

Paired ACTIVITY

4 **Talking about BDD**

With your partner, discuss the following questions.

(a)   Does it surprise you that these celebrities have BDD?

(b)   How important do you think it is that they share their experience of BDD?

(c)   Do you think we have a responsibility to think about how our language and behaviour can seriously affect others?

Social and cultural pressures

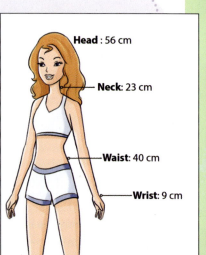

Barbie shocks

In 2013, US website rehabs.com released some shocking statistics showing the impossible physical proportions of the popular fashion doll. If the original Barbie doll was a real-sized woman she would:

- Have a head 5 centimetres larger than average on a neck twice as long and 15 centimetres thinner and so be unable to lift her head
- Have a 40-centimetre waist, leaving room for only half a liver and a few centimetres of intestine
- Have 9-centimetre wrists, 15-centimetre ankles and child-sized feet, which would prevent her from doing any heavy lifting
- Have legs that are 50% longer than her arms – the average woman's legs are only 20% longer
- Be unable to support this uneven weight distribution standing up, so would have to walk on all fours

Head : 56 cm

Neck: 23 cm

Waist: 40 cm

Wrist: 9 cm

Legs: 50% longer than arms

Ankle: 15 cm

Barbie's dimensions

Barbie gets a reality check

In 2016 Mattel transformed their famous doll with new body shapes, skin tones and hair types. Barbie now has three new body types: tall, petite and curvy. These versions will be sold alongside the original model. Mattel had to face the demands for changes in beauty ideals and the ongoing public criticism of Barbie's impossible proportions and remake the doll accordingly.

Models famous for their beauty quirks

| Georgia May Jagger – gapped teeth | Cara Delevingne – heavy eyebrows | Grace Bol – shaved head | Shaun Ross – first male albino model |

> *There is no exquisite beauty … without some strangeness in the proportion.*
>
> Edgar Allan Poe, American writer

> *There are not more than five musical notes, yet the combinations of these five give rise to more melodies than can ever be heard.*
>
> *There are not more than five primary colours, yet in combination they produce more hues than can ever be seen.*
>
> *There are not more than five cardinal tastes (sour, acrid, salt, sweet, bitter), yet combinations of them yield more flavours than can ever be tasted.*
>
> Sun Tzu, The Art of War

As the quotes above illustrate, beauty comes in all shapes and sizes – we are all different and unique. It's our very uniqueness that we should celebrate!

Support

Bodywhys is the national eating disorder association of Ireland. They provide a variety of supports for people affected by eating disorders.

Helpful websites:
www.bodywhys.ie

2. Where am I now?

"*Things can be really empty in this world and I don't mean just the music world. It can become a very meaningless place if you don't really understand: who am I? Why am I here? What am I doing? To feel fulfilment and a deeper level of understanding, personally, that is the most important thing.*"

Alicia Keyes, R&B singer-songwriter, pianist, musician, record producer and actress

We often have misconceptions about where we are in the world. Sometimes we are so busy that we do not see where we really fit into our own lives. So let's take some time to look at the **big picture**! The tips on the next page can help you see where you are in your life right now.

Tips

1. **Recognise your accomplishments.** These accomplishments can range from positive interactions with others, small changes you made or created, difficulties overcome or awards received (remember intrinsic and extrinsic motivations in Module 1, page 9?)

2. **Practise gratitude.** Did you thank your parents for the runners they paid for? Do you show people how much you value the little things they do for you? When you regularly practise giving thanks it helps you stay connected to the right here and now.

3. **Clear out frustrations.** Stop letting little annoying things hang over you: tidy up the mess in your room, do the assignments that have to be done so they will no longer take up any head space. Make a list of all the things you need to do that are bothering you and tackle them one by one. You will feel a great sense of satisfaction when you tick them off.

4. **Create a self-care routine.** When we are under pressure or in a negative mood, we convince ourselves that the last thing we have time for is to stop, think or maybe spend time with friends. But doing an activity we enjoy can shift our mindset into a more positive state.

5. **Exercise.** Take a break from technology – leave your laptop, phone etc. and go for a walk, reconnect with nature and draw some new inspiration from being part of the world. Movement helps you reconnect with the here and now, and the physical energy will shift your mental energy.

6. **Know who supports you**. Make a list of the people in your life who you know you can turn to, relationships that bring happiness to your life. Who are the people you can trust and that encourage you to do your best? Stay away from negative people: their negativity will wear you down.

7. **Remove self-critical voices.** People with low self-esteem listen to the negative voices in their head telling them they are not good enough and should not even try. Again, a shift of mindset can propel a person forward. Don't listen to negative inner voices and turn can't into can. Remember, those nasty negative voices are just thoughts – not the truth.

ACTIVITY

1 **My big picture**

(a) Having read the tips above, it's time to look at your own big picture. Read the instructions for each petal below and write your answers on the petals on page 62.

(i) List four things that you have achieved/accomplished.

(ii) List four things that you are grateful for.

(iii) List four things that you need to do (clear frustrations).

(iv) List four things that you do to take care of yourself.

(v) List four ways in which you get exercise.

(vi) List four people who support you and that you can trust.

(vii) List four negative things that you tell yourself.

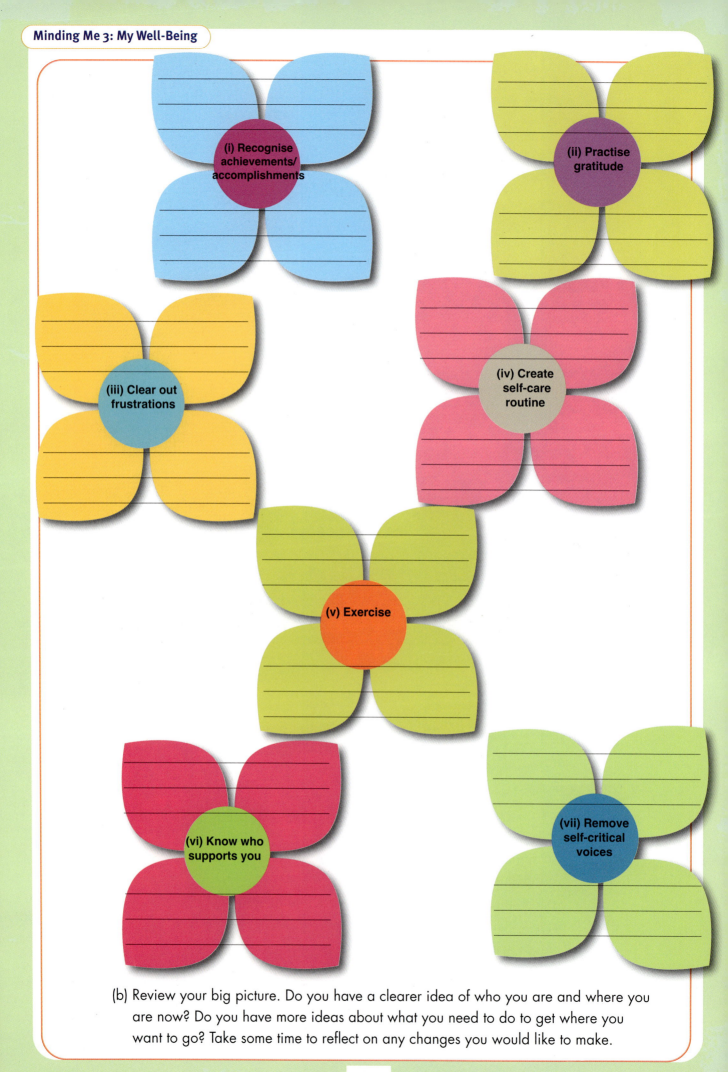

(i) Recognise achievements/accomplishments

(ii) Practise gratitude

(iii) Clear out frustrations

(iv) Create self-care routine

(v) Exercise

(vi) Know who supports you

(vii) Remove self-critical voices

(b) Review your big picture. Do you have a clearer idea of who you are and where you are now? Do you have more ideas about what you need to do to get where you want to go? Take some time to reflect on any changes you would like to make.

Sense of self

There are times in your life when it is a good idea to take stock, to see how you are developing as a person – physically, mentally, emotionally and socially. Adolescence is one of those times on your pathway to adulthood when you have a key opportunity to reflect on your development.

Teenagers with a 'sense of self' seem to enjoy their teens the most. They are more likely to have high self-esteem, have hope for their future and abstain from risky behaviour. A sense of self can be established by having a good mentor in your life, someone to talk to and share ideas with on a regular basis. This mentor could be a parent, an older sibling, a member of the extended family or an older close friend. A good mentor will accept you and guide you through the stages of adolescence. Having a mentor can help you out with the health and lifestyle issues that teenagers are presented with today. (Your mentor could also be your one good adult.)

ACTIVITY

2 **My sense of self**

(a) What do you think having a sense of self means?

_____

(b) Who is your mentor? If you don't have one, who would you like to become your mentor?

_____

'For what it's worth: it's never too late or, in my case, too early to be whoever you want to be. There's no time limit, stop whenever you want. You can change or stay the same; there are no rules to this thing. We can make the best or the worst of it. I hope you make the best of it. And I hope you see things that startle you. I hope you feel things you never felt before. I hope you meet people with a different point of view. I hope you live a life you're proud of. If you find that you're not, I hope you have the courage to start all over again. '

Eric Roth, American screenwriter, The Curious Case of Benjamin Button

3. Relationships: what's important

Throughout your life you will have many relationships. The people we form relationships with generally fall into four categories:

Family   Close friends   Friends   Acquaintances

NOTE
Acquaintances are people you know slightly.

WB1

WB2

ACTIVITY

① **Categorising relationships**

Read the following statements and name who you would contact, why and the kind of relationship you have with that person.

Statement	Who?	Why?	Category
You have just broken up with your boyfriend/girlfriend after being together for six months. You are devastated.			
Your best friend has gone missing from a party and you can't find her to go home.			
You saw a boy taking a mobile phone out of another student's school bag and putting it into his pocket.			
You are not sure where to get the number 19 bus.			
You are finding the workload in school and your sports commitments a bit stressful.			
You want to find out about the school trip.			
You want to help out with the Tidy Towns competition in your area.			
You are so worried about exams that you can't concentrate.			

It is clear from this activity that we rely on different people for different things. Our range of relationships depends on our needs.

The truth about teen relationships on screen

The storylines in television dramas nowadays are often about intense attraction, steamy intimacies and sexual encounters. These dramas are aimed at young people with young actors taking on these roles. It is no wonder that those who watch such shows are led to believe that 'everyone is doing it', when actually they are not.

According to research by the HSE Crisis Pregnancy Programme (CPP), the majority of Irish teens are not having sex before the age of 17.

Other storylines in these shows also illustrate many more fictions such as:

- **Being a virgin is uncool**
  Fact: Most young people see virginity as something to hold onto, not something to get rid of as soon as you can. Being a virgin in the teen years is perfectly normal and it is in fact illegal to have sex before you are 17, even if you consent. Often, however, there is peer pressure within groups to have sex at a young age. The CPP's research shows that those who did have sex at an early age usually did it because of pressure and regretted it afterward.

- **There is no need to talk about contraception in a relationship**
  Fact: The storylines of betrayal, multiple partners and cliffhangers of 'Who's the father?' clearly suggest a lack of responsibility in practising safe sex. Contraception is not talked about in these dramas when the fact is that over 90% of 18–24-year-olds use contraception.

- **Sex can be meaningless**
  Fact: In shows with storylines of multiple partners, the act of sex is seen as a casual action that has no feelings (strings) attached. The fact is every sexual encounter has consequences, from conflicting emotions to some long-term health risks. According to the CPP's website, B4uDecide, it seems that most teens do think that sex is a big deal. 'They want to be in a secure and loving relationship with someone they respect and trust before they have sex.'

Helpful website:
For more facts about sex, check out www.b4udecide.ie.

4. The 3 Rs: respect, rights and responsibilities

In all relationships, it is important to remember the 3 Rs.

If these three attributes are considered, then most relationships will be healthy and rewarding.

Paired ACTIVITY

1 **Should I stay or should I go?**

In pairs, discuss the behaviours listed below. If your boyfriend/girlfriend did any of the following, could you say there was respect in the relationship?

(a) Checks up on me and reads my text messages

(b) Jealous of my friends

(c) Controls me

(d) Gives me orders

(e) Won't accept breaking up

(f) Pressurises me into being physically intimate

(g) Insists I send sexually explicit pictures of myself on my mobile phone

(h) Wants me to buy gifts all the time

ACTIVITY

WB1

WB3

WB4

2 **Healthy relationship guidelines**

In the boxes below, suggest five ways to ensure a romantic relationship is a healthy relationship. A romantic relationship without respect is an unhealthy one.

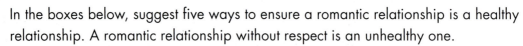

Respect

Group ACTIVITY

Aware

3 **Friendship and privacy**

Read the following conversation between two friends, Cheryl and Jane. In small groups discuss how they deal with the issues of privacy and intimacy.

CHERYL: We saw you and Pete head off together at the party – so what's the story? Are you two going out together now?

JANE: We were together alright, but what else were we supposed to do? Everyone else was with someone.

CHERYL: So what did you get up to?

JANE: We got on fine – he's nice when you get to know him, and he feels just as awkward as I do about the two of us being the only single ones in the gang.

CHERYL: Yeah, he seems nice, but tell me, how far did you go?

JANE: We walked down to the end of the garden.

CHERYL: You know what I mean – did you kiss and stuff?

JANE: I'm not telling you what we did or didn't do – it's none of your business!

CHERYL: Come on! Tell me what you did. Please?

JANE: Everyone knows how far you and Dan have gone. I'm surprised your mam doesn't know, and when she does find out it'll be your own fault for telling everyone.

CHERYL: She'll never find out, so don't worry about that. Go on, I won't tell anyone if you tell me. We're BFFs, aren't we?

JANE: You are my BFF, and if you lay off being nosey and asking all these questions you'll be my super BFF, OK?

CHERYL: K then.

If you read someone else's diary, you get what you deserve.

David Sedaris, author and essayist

Friends don't spy; true friendship is about privacy, too.

Stephen King

Remember!

Can you recall the advice given about sexting in *Minding Me 2: My Well-Being*, Module 6, page 67? Always think before you share.

4 Sexting

Read each of the following statements, then tick the **Agree**, **Disagree** or **Unsure** column in the table below.

Statement	Agree	Disagree	Unsure
If a person is putting pressure on you to send a sext then they don't have your best interests at heart.			
Sexting is something you have to do if you are in a relationship.			
If you have naked images of people under the age of 17 on your phone or computer you could be charged with handling child pornography.			
Parents can never understand the pressures young people are under to send sexts.			
You can't control who sees your photo once it is online.			
Any picture you post online cannot be copied and saved by other people.			
If something is posted on a website with the intention to hurt someone else then you should report it.			

Helpful website:
www.hotline.ie
www.thinkuknow.co.uk
www.b4udecide.ie

NOTE
Hotline.ie provides an anonymous facility for the public to confidentially report suspected illegal content encountered on the Internet. It is run by the Internet Service Providers Association of Ireland in collaboration with An Garda Síochána and the Department of Justice and Equality (Office of Internet Safety).

Respectful language

- Respect can be shown in many different ways, e.g. by listening or by treating people equally.

- The language or the words we use to describe a person or a relationship can sometimes be disrespectful.

- Disrespect is often evident when slang terms, or rude or offensive words, are used to discuss relationships.

Group ACTIVITY

5   **Swearing**

As a class, discuss the following statement:

Young people start swearing because they want to appear more grown up.

✂ **Remember!**

Think about your words before you speak and practise a respectful language law (RLL). See *Minding Me 1: My Well-Being*, Module 6, page 76.

What are rights?

Rights are a list of entitlements that protect how people are treated. They are used to ensure equality and fair treatment. There are many different forms of rights: welfare rights, political rights, animal rights, legal rights and personal rights.

Nobody can take a right away from you. It is yours and is meant to protect you and help you reach your full potential in life.

✂ Remember!

In CSPE you may have read about the Universal Declaration of Human Rights (UDHR) and the United Nations Convention on the Rights of the Child (UNCRC).

ACTIVITY

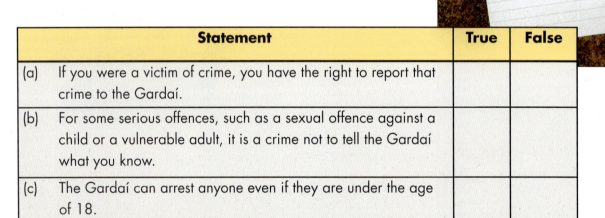

6 **Do you know your rights?**

Read the following statements and tick whether you think they are true or false.

Statement	True	False
(a) If you were a victim of crime, you have the right to report that crime to the Gardaí.		
(b) For some serious offences, such as a sexual offence against a child or a vulnerable adult, it is a crime not to tell the Gardaí what you know.		
(c) The Gardaí can arrest anyone even if they are under the age of 18.		
(d) It is not against the law to leave school before you are 16 years of age.		
(e) You have automatic parental rights if you are an unmarried father.		
(f) No matter what age you are, you have the right to be protected from all forms of abuse and exploitation.		

TRB

Statement		True	False
(g)	You have a right to free dental services up to the age of 15 years, if you are attending school.		
(h)	You must be aged 18 to consent to mental health treatment.		
(i)	Legally, you can consent to sex at 17. This is the same irrespective of your sexual orientation – whether you are heterosexual, gay, lesbian or bisexual.		
(j)	There is no age restriction on buying condoms.		
(k)	You are not entitled to continue your education if you are pregnant.		
(l)	You have the right to be protected from discrimination at school, when you buy or sell something, when you use a service such as the bus, attend a youth or sports group, or when you are in employment.		
(m)	Neighbours have the right to complain about young people hanging around the neighbourhood if they find the behaviour disruptive.		
(n)	It is illegal for anyone under 18 to buy or to possess alcohol.		
(o)	It is illegal for a shop to sell tobacco products to anyone under the age of 18, but it is OK if they are for someone else.		
(p)	You can drive a motorcycle, moped or tractor when you are 16, but you must be 17 to drive a car.		

Helpful website:

www.citizensinformation.ie

You can find out more about your rights if you've been a victim of crime or when dealing with the Gardaí. Check out the Children and Young People section of the Irish Council for Civil Liberties' Know Your Rights guide to criminal justice and Garda powers, at www.knowyourrights.ie.

 WB1

 WB3

7 **Rights and relationships**

You have learned a lot about young people's rights for inclusion in society, but how much do you know about young people's rights and responsibilities in a personal relationship?

In the table below list the rights and responsibilities you can think of in a personal relationship.

Rights	Responsibilities

 Remember!

One of the most fundamental rights a person has in a relationship is the right to say no.

Right to sexuality

The right to sexuality is the freedom to express any element of one's sexuality. Similar to the rights freely expressed by heterosexuals, it includes the right for homosexuals and bisexuals to be free from discrimination on the grounds of sexual orientation. It protects the rights of all sexual orientations, such as lesbian, gay, bisexual and heterosexual. These rights belong to every person.

Remember!

We looked at sexual orientations in *Minding Me 1: My Well-Being*, Module 6, page 80.

'Have any of you ever come home in the evening, and turned on the television and there are a panel of people, respectable people, smart people, the kind of people who probably make good neighbourly neighbours, the kind of people who write for newspapers. And they are all sitting around and they are having a reasoned debate, about you and about what kind of person you are, about whether or not you are capable of being a good parent, about whether you want to destroy marriage, about whether or not you are safe around children, about whether or not God herself thinks you are an abomination (a disgrace), about whether or not you are "intrinsically disordered". And even the nice TV presenter lady, that you feel is almost a friend because you see her being nice on TV all the time, even she thinks it's perfectly OK that they are all having this reasoned debate about you, and about who you are, and about what rights you "deserve" or don't deserve. And that feels oppressive.'

The above quote is from the Noble Call speech by Rory O'Neill aka Panti Bliss given in the Abbey Theatre, Dublin, before the same-sex marriage referendum in Ireland in 2015, a speech which helped to shift attitudes in Ireland and around the world.

Paired ACTIVITY

8 **Discussion**

In pairs, discuss the following questions.

(a) If we believe that showing your feelings towards a romantic partner is a basic right regardless of whether you are gay or straight, do you think couples should show their romantic feelings in public in a different way depending on whether the couple is straight or gay?

(b) Do you think the media is more biased towards one sexual preference than others? Explain why you think so.

(c) Irish politician Leo Varadkar publicly announced on Irish radio that he is gay. 'It is not something that defines me,' he said. What do you think he meant by that?

(d) Do you think that all people in positions of authority should declare their sexual orientation/preference?

WB1

WB2

WB3

WB4

Republic of Equals

TRB

NOTE

On 22 May 2015 the Republic of Ireland became the first country in the world to approve same-sex marriage by popular vote.

Teenage pregnancy

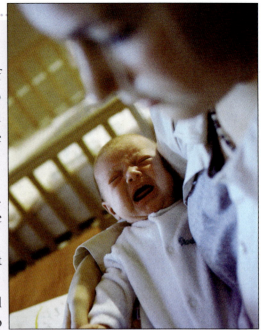

Once a girl has her first period, her body is capable of having a baby. Although the majority of adolescents do not enter into a physically intimate relationship until they are older, some do and a number of these encounters can lead to teenage pregnancy.

- Being a father or mother to a new baby can be tough. It may be a stressful time, with things not going the way you thought they would.

- Sometimes it can be difficult to talk to those closest to you but talking to a counsellor can help.

- According to the latest information from the Central Statistics Office, the total number of births to teenagers has decreased from 3,087 in 2001 to 1,253 in 2014, a decline of 60% over 13 years.

- A sexually active teen who doesn't use contraceptives has a 90% chance of becoming pregnant within a year.

- A teenage girl may try to hide a pregnancy and fail to get medical help, which can have implications for both the mother and the unborn child.

- A father's rights are particular to his situation: for example they are different if he is married to the baby's mother or living with her or has no contact at all.

Helen Deely, Head of the HSE Sexual Health & Crisis Pregnancy Programme, said: 'There has been a significant shift in our society over the last 14 years … Relationships and Sexuality Education in schools and youth groups has a huge part to play in the figures outlined today with research showing that those who received sex education were 1.5 times more likely to have used contraception the first time they had sex compared to those who did not receive sex education.'

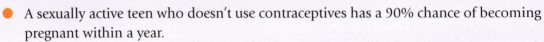

ACTIVITY

 9   **Personal research**

Check out the facts and real stories about becoming a young parent at:
www.reachout.com
www.b4udecide.ie
www.cura.ie

(10) **Problem page**

Dear _____ (your one good adult),
I am 15 years old and I have just discovered I am pregnant. I am confused and I don't know what to do. I only slept with my boyfriend once and he isn't my boyfriend anymore; we broke up two months ago. I drank too much at a party and on the way home he suggested we have sex and we used a condom. Now I'm pregnant.

Nobody knows I'm pregnant and I'm trying to hide my bump, but I am getting bigger each week. I don't know if I want this baby or not. I don't feel I'm ready and I cry all the time. If my parents found out, I think they would tell me to leave home and they would be very angry.

I had a plan, a dream of going to college to be a vet and then going to work in a wildlife park in Kenya, but if I have a baby this won't happen. I feel my life is ruined. What should I do?

Penny

Respond to Penny as each of the following people who might help her in her life. Remember to refer to the physical, emotional, social, moral and financial implications in your answer.

(a) as her ex-boyfriend: _____

_____

_____

_____

_____

_____

_____

_____

_____

(b) as her parents: _____

_____

_____

_____

_____

_____

_____

_____

_____

_____

(c)   as her best friend: _____

_____

_____

_____

_____

_____

_____

_____

_____

(d)   as her doctor: _____

_____

_____

_____

_____

_____

_____

_____

_____

_____

5. Conflict

All relationships experience conflict at some time, but it is how this conflict is resolved that is important.

Conflict can often occur when people have a clash of opinions. Both may feel that their opinions are not being respected and they may feel hurt because of this.

 Remember!

We looked at communication in situations of conflict in *Module 3: Communication Skills*, pages 30–32.

1 **Sources of conflict**

List some typical sources of conflict in the following relationships.

Parents	
Friends	
Boyfriend/Girlfriend	

The best and simplest way to deal with conflict is to respect the other person and listen to what they are saying. State how you feel about the situation and then try to discuss possible options or solutions to the problem that you will both be happy to accept.

2 **Resolution**

(a)   Think about a conflict you have encountered in a relationship and how you dealt with it, then fill in the table below.

Conflict	How did you deal with it?	What could you have done better?

(b)   When you have completed the table, share and discuss it with the person next to you.

End of Module Review

Looking back on the activities you took part in and what you learned in this module, answer the following questions.

(a)   Which activity did you like the most and why?

_____

_____

_____

_____

(b)   Which activity, if any, did you dislike and why?

_____

_____

_____

_____

(c)   What would you like to learn more about?

_____

_____

_____

_____

Module 7

Emotional Health

In this module we will learn about our feelings and moods and how they can affect us. We will look specifically at what stress is and how we can help reduce stress levels in our everyday lives.

 Digital Resources are available for this module at mentorbooks.ie/resources

We will explore:

1. Feelings and moods

Managing our emotional health is just as important as managing our physical health. Each boosts the other to give you that 'good all over' feeling. Exercise relieves the muscular symptoms of stress and releases endorphins in the brain, which make us feel good. Keeping active maintains a zest for life, whereas doing very little activity makes us feel more moody, tired and irritable.

Becoming accustomed to the many new feelings, moods and experiences of adolescence can feel overwhelming at times. It is important to remember that with all the physical changes occurring, keeping a lid on it is not always easy!

Some teenagers can be too hard on themselves during this time. They compare themselves to others and often find themselves full of flaws. Others enjoy the changes and challenges ahead of them and see themselves as just as capable as the next person. It all depends on your outlook.

Mood

While we often hear the term **mood**, what exactly does it mean to be in a mood? A mood can be made up of a number of parts: a feeling, a thought and an action. If you are in a happy mood you will probably be feeling happy, thinking happy thoughts and laughing or smiling.

Our mood can be like a lens through which we view other aspects of our life, and our perception of events can be altered because of our mood. If you are in an angry mood and something you don't like is said or suggested to you, you will more than likely have a stronger reaction than if you were in a happy mood.

1 Reactions

Marie tells her best friend Rita that she needs to change the cinema time for tonight as she has to be home earlier than planned.

(a) Imagine Rita is in a good mood – what do you think her response to Marie will be?

_____

_____

_____

(b) Imagine Rita is in a discouraged mood – what will her response to Marie be?

_____

_____

_____

We often use the term bad mood to describe what are actually feelings of unhappiness or sadness.

If you are in a negative mood, a couple of things which might help you are:

- **Talking about it:** if you speak to someone about what is worrying you, it might help you to feel better. People usually feel more positive after someone has listened to them.
- **An attitude of gratitude:** thinking of the glass as half-full can have a positive impact on your well-being. During adolescence, it can be helpful to keep a gratitude journal and each day write five things you are grateful for, e.g. I really enjoyed my breakfast this morning; I am looking forward to visiting my cousins today etc.
- **Labelling your emotion:** think about how you feel. You may discover that when you really think about it, you feel sad rather than angry, or disappointed rather than resentful. It can be useful to label your emotion as it makes it easier to think of how to address the problem causing the emotion.

2 **What I am grateful for**

WB4

In the space below, write five things you are grateful for today.

(a) _____

(b) _____

(c) _____

(d) _____

(e) _____

👉 **Remember!**

Mantras are words or phrases you can say to yourself in a difficult situation to help you deal with that situation.

3 **Mantras**

(a) Can you think of a slogan you might use to help you when you are feeling in a bad mood?

_____

_____

(b) Can you think of a slogan you might use if you are feeling pressure during a presentation/assignment? This could be your mantra.

_____

_____

Aware

Self-talk

WB4

Self-talk can be a very useful skill for young people. Positive self-talk can help a young person feel better about themselves and build resilience (the ability to recover quickly), but negative self-talk can result in a young person feeling emotional and not coping with issues that might be happening in their life.

👉 **Remember!**

Self-talk is what we say to ourselves – generally inside our head but sometimes out loud.

ACTIVITY

4 **Positive/negative**

Give an example of **positive self-talk** and **negative self-talk** for each of the following situations.

(a)   Laura is the only person from her class going on the school ski trip.
   (i)   Positive self-talk

   _____

   (ii)   Negative self-talk

   _____

(b)   Jade is baking a special birthday cake for her dad.
   (i)   Positive self-talk

   _____

   (ii)   Negative self-talk

   _____

(c)   Johnny is handing in his first exam assignment.
   (i)   Positive self-talk

   _____

   (ii)   Negative self-talk

   _____

(d)   Orla is going to her cousin's 16th birthday party in Galway but she doesn't know most of the other people going.
   (i)   Positive self-talk

   _____

   (ii)   Negative self-talk

   _____

(e)   In the above situations, what impact could the negative self-talk have on these people?

   _____

   _____

(f)   Why do you think it's important to use positive self-talk?

   _____

   _____

At times when you may be inclined towards negative self-talk, adapt the following to fit your situation:

- I am … (confident, efficient, kind, strong, etc.)
- I can … (try to score a goal, finish my assignment, give it my best etc.)
- I will … (do my homework, go to the party anyway, say I'm sorry, ask for help etc.)

If you practise the above you will become a lot more comfortable with using positive self-talk, and this will have an impact on your mood and how you feel about yourself.

Handling emotions

Some new emotions that may surface during adolescence are attraction, independence, insecurity and awkwardness.

Suggestions to deal with new or strong emotions

- Take a moment to recognise the feeling you have (e.g. anger, shyness, etc.).

- Identify where you are feeling that emotion most in your body (e.g. shoulders, chest, stomach).

- Accept it as your own emotion/feeling.

- If it is positive, decide on the best method to express that particular feeling.

- If the feeling is negative, question what it was that triggered this feeling in you. Did someone say something negative to you (external influence)? Are you setting targets for yourself that are unrealistic (internal influence)? Is this a familiar feeling that you think you may need to talk to someone about?

Handling emotions involves checking-in with ourselves **before** we act on them. Regular checking-in with ourselves boosts our emotional health significantly. It provides us with the opportunity to find out what is going on inside ourselves, so we can decide if the feeling is something we need to act upon or not.

Be sure to check in with yourself at the start of the next mood swing!

NOTE
The more familiar we become with our own feelings, the better we will be at recognising the feelings of others. This interpersonal skill is found in the most successful managers and leaders.

 Remember!

Expressing your feelings has many health benefits: it reduces stress, eases anxiety and helps share happiness.

5 **Mood sheet for one day**

To catalogue (make a list of) your moods and feelings from the previous day, make a dot on the table below for each time of the day. The dot should also be in line with the word that best describes how you felt at that time of day. Join the dots to make a graph displaying your mood changes for that day.

Emotions	8 a.m.	11 a.m.	1 p.m.	4 p.m.	6 p.m.	8 p.m.	10 p.m.
Confident							
Assertive							
Positive							
Excited							
Interactive							
Giddy							
Cheerful							
Content							
Relaxed							
Calm							
Quiet							
Worried							
Stressed							
Apathetic							
Bored							
Negative							
Afraid							
Grumpy							
Angry							
Withdrawn							
Lonely							
Sad							

From the graph on the previous page, select one positive emotion and one negative emotion that you have experienced and answer the following questions:

Question	Negative emotion	Positive emotion
1. Name the emotion.		
2. What external or internal factors led you to feel this emotion?		
3. What behaviour did you use to express this emotion?		
4. Do you think you expressed that emotion appropriately?		
5. If you felt that way again, what method of expression would you use?		

2. Stress

Stress can mean different things to different people. One person's level of stress could be very different to another person's given the same set of circumstances.

Stress is a feeling that's created when you react to certain events. It's the body's way of preparing to meet a tough situation. Some people perform better under stress as they feel it gives them extra focus, strength, stamina and heightened alertness. For others it may be more overwhelming, causing mood swings, irritation or the urge to run away and hide, which if not dealt with could cause health problems and depression.

TRB

Helpful website:
www.reachout.com

1 **Stressful situations**

Many things can cause a young person to be stressed. In small groups, describe five situations that you think a young person might find stressful.

(a) _____

(b) _____

(c) _____

(d) _____

(e) _____

We tend to focus our attention on the situations in life that cause us stress. It can be helpful to focus on the times we dealt well with stressful situations and try to learn from them.

ACTIVITY

2 **Dealing with stress successfully**

(a) Think of a time you dealt with a stressful situation well. Explain what happened.

_____

_____

_____

_____

(b) What did you do that helped you deal so well with the issue at hand – e.g. did you talk to a friend? Did you just try to think about it positively?

_____

_____

_____

_____

Stressors

Anything that causes stress is termed a **stressor**. There are three main categories of stressor:

- **Environmental stressors:** These include heat, noise, overcrowding, climate and terrain.

- **Physiological stressors:** These can be drugs, caffeine, tobacco, injury, infection, disease or physical effort.

- **Emotional (psychosocial) stressors:** In this category we include any life-changing event, e.g. family illness, conflict, death of a family member or friend and increased responsibility. In school, pressures regarding grades or deadlines for projects or presentations may cause stress.

It is important to be able to recognise when you are stressed and to identify your triggers, as this can allow your body and mind to prepare for the situation.

3 Recognising stress

(a) The table below describes typical indicators of someone under stress. Tick each reaction as either an internal or external expression of stress.

	Internal	External
Gritting teeth		
Headache		
Hunching shoulders		
White knuckles		
Sweating		
Biting fingernails		
Heart beating faster		
Mouth dry		
Back pain		
Tapping foot		

(b) Do you have any experience of the above expressions of stress? Can you identify how you got to that stage of stress?

_____

_____

Too much stress can result in mental or physical diseases. Such diseases include: high blood pressure, heart disease, depression, colitis, ulcers, headaches, insomnia, constipation, diarrhoea and back pain. With too much stress we 'burn out'.

NOTE
There is good stress and there is bad stress.

Too little stress, or 'rust out', is not good for our health either. Moderate stress levels are considered good for healthy growth and maturity. Some stress is necessary to keep you excited about life, e.g. winning a race, a rollercoaster ride, watching a scary movie. The right amount of stress is known as **eustress**.

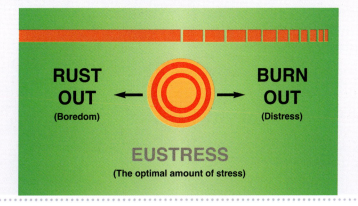

ACTIVITY

4 **Levels of stress**

(a) Can you list situations where rust out, eustress and burn out might happen in your typical week?

(i) Rust out: _____

(ii) Eustress: _____

(iii) Burn out: _____

(b) What do you think rust out feels like?

_____

(c) Draw an emoticon to capture the perfect amount of stress.

[ ]

(d) How would you recognise if you were suffering from burn out?

_____

Five steps to manage stress levels

1. First identify the **situations** in your life that make you stressed.

2. Identify the area of your **body** where you are holding this stress.

3. Next, use some type of **relaxation** technique to relieve the symptoms, e.g. meditation.

4. Try to **avoid** some of the stressors in your life.

5. Finally, take **exercise**. The fitter you are, the better you will be able to cope with stress.

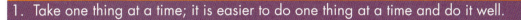

Tips for managing stress

WB1

1. Take one thing at a time; it is easier to do one thing at a time and do it well.

2. Take action instead of worrying about something; you may need to leave the situation or tackle the task again later.

3. If you cannot come up with a solution, try to accept the situation by changing your feelings about it. If you are feeling overwhelmed, take a few deep breaths to calm you down.

4. Think positively – visualise yourself succeeding.

5. Look at stressors as challenges – use the adrenaline to get you started.

6. Don't let little things bother you – stay focused.

7. Prioritise your tasks – do what is most urgent first.

8. Balance work with rest and play.

9. Make sure you have support from home, friends and family.

Paired ACTIVITY

5 Advice

The following problems are from a web forum where young people can post about situations they are finding stressful and other young people can try to advise them. For each of the situations below, can you and your partner (i) identify what is causing the stress; (ii) offer a way in which this person might reduce their stress level; (iii) suggest how they might avoid similar stress in the future.

(a)

Hi there,

I'm writing here because I don't know what else to do – everyone thinks I'm sorted and OK, but I'm not. I smile on the outside but inside I don't know how I get through some days. I'm in school with all my assignments and exams to do; I'm in the school choir, on the school football team and the team in my parish. I help on my grandad's farm at the weekends, as he's getting older now. I don't have time to eat, really, or I eat in the car or bus when I'm travelling. I never see my friends – I don't even have time to text them sometimes. I have headaches and stomach pain but I don't have time to be sick. Has this happened to anyone else? What should I do?

(i) Cause of stress: _____

_____

(ii) Way to reduce stress: _____

_____

(iii) How to avoid stress: _____

_____

(b)

Hi there,

My parents are separating and I can't stop thinking about it. Who I will live with? Will I see my other parent? What about my grandparents and cousins? I can't sleep – I toss and turn all night then I can't stay awake in school. I can't eat. I really am desperate for advice, please. What should I do?

(i) Cause of stress: _____

(ii) Way to reduce stress: _____

(iii) How to avoid stress: _____

> 'The greatest weapon against stress is our ability to choose one thought over another. '
>
> **William James**

> 'Life is really simple, but we insist on making it complicated.'
>
> **Confucius**

End of Module Review

As a class group, brainstorm what information or tips you think would be useful for other students in the school to have about stress. The resulting list could be posted on a noticeboard or your school's website.

Module 8
Influences and Decisions

In Module 8 of *Minding Me 2: My Well-Being* you learned about positive and negative influences, as well as making decisions. You have also been building positive communication skills in all three *Minding Me* books. We will now look at how to make life choices. These are serious choices that will impact on your life now and in the future. It is really important to learn how to make good decisions when faced with these types of choices.

 Digital Resources are available for this module at mentorbooks.ie/resources

We will explore:

1. Choice-making

1   **The Road Not Taken**

'The Road Not Taken'
by Robert Frost

Two roads diverged in a yellow wood,
And sorry I could not travel both
And be one traveller, long I stood
And looked down one as far as I could
To where it bent in the undergrowth;

Then took the other, as just as fair,
And having perhaps the better claim,
Because it was grassy and wanted wear;
Though as for that the passing there
Had worn them really about the same,

And both that morning equally lay
In leaves no step had trodden black.
Oh, I kept the first for another day!
Yet knowing how way leads on to way,
I doubted if I should ever come back.

I shall be telling this with a sigh
Somewhere ages and ages hence:
Two roads diverged in a wood, and I –
I took the one less travelled by,
And that has made all the difference.

(a)   Which letter in line 1 might represent the forked road?

_____

(b)   What do you think the 'undergrowth' represents (line 5)?

_____

(c)   What motivates or encourages the speaker when he makes his choice?

_____

(d)   How do you interpret the last line of the poem?

_____

_____

(e)   Write five lines about a time when you took a less-travelled road.

_____

_____

_____

_____

_____

Throughout your life, you will have many choices to make. Some of these will have a huge impact on the direction your life takes (e.g. to work abroad, to get married); others less so (where to go on holidays, which phone to buy). Later on, we will look at how you might go about choosing a career. But now let's look at a more immediate choice facing you!

2   **Fifth-Year subject choices**

Think about the subject options you're taking in Junior Cycle and fill out the table below. This should give you a good idea of how you feel about these subjects and whether you want to keep them on for Leaving Cert.

Subjects for Junior Cycle	Predicted grades for final exam in Junior Cycle based on pre-results (be realistic!)	Do I like this subject? (Yes/no/undecided)	Would this be a good choice for my Leaving Cert? (Yes/no/undecided)
(a)			
(b)			
(c)			
(d)			
(e)			
(f)			
(g)			
(h)			
(i)			

Decisions about personal issues are addressed in *Module 6: Relationships and Sexuality Education* and *Module 7: Emotional Health*. The social issues are addressed in *Module 3: Communication Skills*, *Module 5: Friendship* and *Module 9: Substance Use*. Reviewing these modules will help inform you before you make your decisions on related issues.

Group ACTIVITY

WB2

3 **Three important choices: Think–Group–Share**

(a) **Round 1:** Working on your own, write down four choices teenagers might have to make in Third Year – whether at home, in school or with friends. Write down each choice on a different piece of paper. You have four minutes to do this.

(b) **Round 2:** In small groups, spread out everyone's four ideas on the table and check if any are duplicated (i.e. more than one person had the same idea). Just keep one version of each idea.

(c) **Round 3 – importance of choices:** Will these choices have a short-term effect (S) or a long-term effect (L) on your lives? Mark each with either S or L.

(d) **Round 4 – categories:** Decide on three suitable headings and group each choice under the relevant one. Think carefully about the headings. Next, fill in the table on the next page, putting each choice under your chosen heading. Don't forget to include the relevant codes from Round 3 (S or L).

Hint: If making a curry, we could group ingredients under three headings – meats/vegetables/spices.

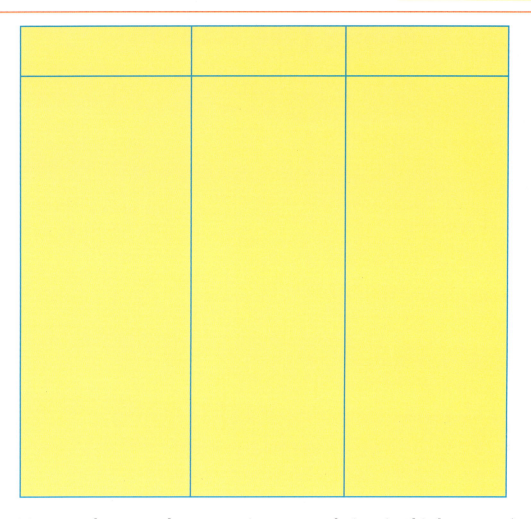

(e) **Round 5 – our three most important choices in Third Year:** Looking at the table, decide as a group which choice you see as most important under each heading and highlight it. Have one person from each group report their three important choices to the whole class.

2. Making good decisions

1 **The seven steps in making a good decision**

For this, we are using the example of choosing a future career.

Step 1: Brainstorm

First think of a person whose job you would really like. Write down why this job appeals to you.

_____

_____

_____

Step 2: Investigate

Use the six journalist's questions to investigate online all aspects of this career:

(a) Who? _____

_____

(b) What? _____

_____

(c) When? _____

_____

(d) Where? _____

_____

(e) Why? _____

_____

(f) How? _____

_____

Step 3: Self-assessment

Self-assessment will help you to find out how suited you are to your career choice. To see if you have the right personality for the job, start by thinking about the things that you are good at, that you enjoy and that motivate you. The headings below will guide you. Answer as honestly as possible.

(a)   List the things that you do well. What do other people praise you for?

_____

_____

_____

(b)   List the things that you enjoy doing. What motivates you? (Remember the 'My motivations' activity from *Module 1: Belonging and Integrating*, page 10.)

_____

_____

_____

(c)   Do you prefer working on your own or working in teams?

_____

Step 4: Reality check

Knowing the type of personality you have will guide you to make realistic plans. It would be very unrealistic to think you can become a doctor when you dislike reading/studying or be a good landscape gardener when you hate the outdoors.

It is also a good idea to check if there is a demand for employees in your chosen area. Check if such jobs will be available by the time you leave school or college and research the career development opportunities.

Look online and read newspapers and magazines to see if you can find any references to this career. Business papers and listings of job vacancies are a good place to start.

Step 5: Interview

Interview someone you know who is in this career. Use the following questions as guidelines in your interview.

- Why did you choose this career?
- What courses did you do to get into this career?
- What are the typical earnings for this career?
- What is the most exciting thing about this career?
- What is the hardest part/downside of the career?
- What are the career development opportunities?
- What are the travel opportunities, if any, of this career?

Talking to adults, neighbours, etc. in your chosen profession is known as networking. It shows your interest in and positive attitude to the job. Networking can help you discover the possibilities of doing some work experience and the names of people to contact in that job. This will also give you more insight into the job and help you decide whether you might like to pursue it as a career.

Step 6: Research

Bearing in mind the qualifications and skills necessary for your chosen career, use the Internet to look up college prospectuses or ask your career guidance teacher for information. Fill in the information in the table below and use it to assess your suitability for the careers you are interested in.

Course name	Name and address of college	Subjects needed/other requirements	Subjects studied in First Year of the course	Duration of the course	Qualification received	Cost

Step 7: Making a good decision

"Knowledge is power."
Sir Francis Bacon, 1561–1626

You need to know your strengths, your likes and your dislikes to tackle most decisions, and you need to gather information on your preferred career to make sure it is the right career for you.

Putting all this knowledge together will aid you in making a good decision. Making a good decision requires thinking ahead.

The research you have just done may inform your choice of subjects for Transition Year and Leaving Certificate or for Leaving Certificate Applied.

If you are still unsure, then it's back to the drawing board. Follow Steps 1 to 7 for another choice of career …

"The only place you will find success before work is in the dictionary."
May B. Smith

End of Module Review

NOTE You do not have to be good at drawing!

Draw images/stickmen/emoticons to help you remember the seven steps in making a good decision.

Step 1: Brainstorm

Step 2: Investigate

Step 3: Self-assessment

Step 4: Reality check

Step 5: Interview

Step 6: Research

Step 7: Making a good decision

Module 9

Substance Use

In this module we will examine the impact of drug addiction on the individual and society. We will also revisit alcohol use and investigate other types of drugs.

 Digital Resources are available for this module at mentorbooks.ie/resources

We will explore:

1. Drug use

Why do young people use drugs/begin to use drugs?

There is a huge bank of international evidence that highlights the negative impact substance use can have on our bodies and particularly the teenage brain. This information is widely available in many different media but still young people continue to misuse drugs and alcohol. While initially a young person may only be experimenting, it doesn't take long before they can become addicted to the substance and this can have a huge impact on the shape of their lives as a teenager and an adult. (See *Module 4: Physical Health*.)

Some of the reasons given in research as to why young people use drugs are outlined below:
- To relax
- To forget about my problems
- To get high
- To rebel
- To try it out
- To feel older than my friends
- To fit in and to feel I belong
- Boredom
- It looks like fun

WB1

1 **Positive alternatives**

In small groups, look at the reasons below for drug use and try to generate a positive alternative way to address each one. For example, 'to relax': is drug use the only way to relax? What other activities could you engage in that would not have a negative effect on your health and well-being?

Reason	Alternative
To relax	
To forget about my problems	
To get high	
To rebel	
To try it out	
To feel older than my friends	
To fit in and to feel I belong	
Boredom	
It looks like fun	

2 **Negative peer pressure**

Case Study 1

Mary is at Martha's house and it is raining – they are bored. Martha goes downstairs and comes back up with a packet of tablets, Xanax. Martha hands one to Mary and tells her it will make her feel good. Mary doesn't want to take it.

What can she say/do? Complete the story from Mary's point of view.

_____
_____
_____
_____
_____
_____
_____

Case Study 2

Mark's older brother Liam is left in charge when their parents go away. Liam is going out to a party and brings Mark along. Liam leaves Mark in the computer room and tells him to play games. James, a boy from Mark's school, is there too. His big sister brought him along as well. After a while Mark and James get bored and go out to the party. Mark starts talking to some people and then James comes over and offers him a white pill in front of these older students. Mark doesn't want it but doesn't know what to do.

Complete the story from Mark's point of view.

_____

_____

_____

_____

_____

_____

_____

The drug-refusal skills needed in the above situations are skills that you may need to draw on at many times in your life. However, for teenagers, negative peer pressure can result in experimenting with and becoming addicted to drugs.

2. Drug addiction

Being addicted to drugs means that you take drugs on a very regular basis and you feel unwell if you do not take them. All drugs – legal and illegal – can become addictive.

Some drugs are more addictive than others – the drug you use and your reason for taking it can influence whether you become addicted or not.

Signs of addiction can include:
- Feeling the need to use the drug regularly
- Having a constant supply of the drug
- Inability to stop using the drug
- Changes in behaviour e.g. stealing, missing school or work

Drug addiction is a serious illness. People who take drugs are called users. Drug addiction can have the following consequences:
- Loneliness
- Homelessness
- Mental illness
- Physical illness or even death
- Stealing to support the habit
- Jail sentence and/or criminal record
- Absenteeism from school or work
- Loss of self-respect and ambition
- Emotional immaturity (if addiction started in the teenage years)
- Prostitution

1   Why?

Choose five consequences from the list on the previous page and explain why you think they happen as a result of drug addiction.

(a) _____

(b) _____

(c) _____

(d) _____

(e) _____

2   Profile

(a) Write a profile/draw a picture of what you think a typical drug user would be like. Consider the following when creating your profile: home, employment, social life, family, education etc.

(b) Compare your profile with those of your classmates. Are there similarities? Is there a stereotypical image of a drug user?

The typical drug addict in today's society doesn't really exist, as people from all socioeconomic backgrounds and different family and educational backgrounds become addicted to drugs. A person's experience of life situations, how they deal with these and the availability of drugs are the main reasons why someone can become addicted to a substance.

3. Alcohol

Paired ACTIVITY

1 **What we've learned**

(a) With your partner, list three pieces of information you remember about alcohol and drinking from *Minding Me 1: My Well-Being* or from your general knowledge.

(i) _____

(ii) _____

(iii) _____

(b) Young people often binge drink, which is harmful and can lead to addiction. Can you describe what binge drinking is?

_____

_____

2 **How much is too much?**

How many drinks do you think could cause the effects of alcohol consumption listed in the table below? Tick the relevant column for each effect.

Effect	0–2 drinks	3–5 drinks	5 drinks or more
(a) Lack of concentration			
(b) Inability to drive			
(c) Pass out			
(d) Inability to make a phone call			
(e) Feel good about yourself			
(f) Take increased risks			
(g) Use other drugs			
(h) Have unsafe sex			
(i) Go to the toilet frequently			
(j) Become aggressive			
(k) Vomit			
(l) Feel relaxed			
(m) Slur speech			
(n) Be injured			

TRB

How many times did you tick '5 drinks or more'? It might surprise you to learn that in all cases, any amount of alcohol can result in negative effects.

Even a small amount of alcohol will result in changes in your behaviour and mental state. Blood alcohol concentration (BAC) refers to the amount of alcohol in a person's bloodstream. Alcohol is absorbed from the small intestine into the bloodstream very quickly as it doesn't require digestion.

It takes your body about one hour to metabolise (break down) one unit of alcohol. The following will have an impact on how your body processes alcohol:

- What weight you are
- If you have eaten
- If you are tired
- Your gender
- How quickly you drank
- If you are taking medication

Most of us, throughout our lives, will be in situations where alcohol is available so it is important to make sensible decisions regarding alcohol consumption.

3 **My experience**

(a) Look at the statements below and indicate whether they apply to you or not.

Statements	Yes	No
(i) You've been in a pub		
(ii) Your friends drink alcohol		
(iii) You've seen ads for alcohol		
(iv) You know the name of five different brands of alcohol		
(v) You've never tasted alcohol		
(vi) You've seen documentaries about the dangers of alcohol		
(vii) You've bought alcohol		
(viii) Someone else has bought alcohol for you		
(ix) Someone in your life is drinking too much and it is impacting their life and your life		

NOTE
Please tell your one good adult if you need help in coping with someone in your life who is abusing alcohol. They can guide you on the next steps to take. You do not need to feel alone.

(b) Now look at the same types of statements listed below but applied to ecstasy/cannabis instead of alcohol. How would you answer these?

Statements		Yes	No
(i)	You've been in a public place where ecstasy/cannabis was being used		
(ii)	Your friends use ecstasy/cannabis		
(iii)	You've seen ads for ecstasy/cannabis		
(iv)	You know the name of five different types of ecstasy/cannabis		
(v)	You've never used ecstasy/cannabis		
(vi)	You've seen documentaries about the dangers of ecstasy/cannabis		
(vii)	You've bought ecstasy/cannabis		
(viii)	Someone else has bought ecstasy/cannabis for you		
(ix)	Someone in your life is using ecstasy/cannabis too much and it is impacting their life and your life		

(c) Look at the similarities and differences between your answers for both tables. Do you think one activity is more socially acceptable than the other?

_____

_____

(d) Why do you think this?

_____

_____

NOTE
Most experts agree that if you spend time with people the same age who take drugs, then it is much more likely that you too will take drugs.

4. Ecstasy

What is ecstasy?

Ecstasy is a hallucinogenic (a drug that can make you lose track of time and where you are; it can lead you to lose your sense of reality) amphetamine. MDMA is an abbreviation of its chemical name, methylenedioxymethamphetamine.

Ecstasy comes in tablet form. It is not manufactured by the pharmaceutical industry, which means it is made illegally. The tablets can often contain other substances, e.g. flour, rat poison, brewer's tablets or paracetamol. This is very dangerous and can lead to death.

1 Definitions

Find out what the following words mean.

(a) Lethargy: _____

(b) Psychological dependence: _____

(c) Depression: _____

(d) Amphetamine: _____

Effects of ecstasy on the body

- Increased heart rate and blood pressure
- Increased body temperature from 37°C to 41°C
- Sweating and dehydration, which can lead to death
- Convulsions
- Brain damage
- Anxiety and panic attacks
- Depression
- Psychological dependence
- Insomnia and lethargy
- Loss of appetite and weight
- Heat stroke
- Blood clotting
- Asthma attacks

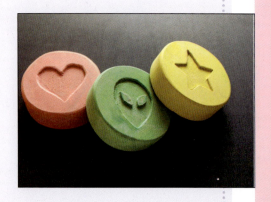

Ecstasy is often associated with nightclubs and parties. In Ireland it is normally sold as a small tablet – the colours can be pink, brown, red or green as well as white. There are generally logos or designs on the surface of the tablet.

Do people die from using ecstasy?

Young people have died from taking just one ecstasy tablet.

How?

- As a result of dehydration: the combination of taking ecstasy, over-sweating from dancing and not drinking enough water can result in heat stroke and death.
- People can overdose on ecstasy tablets.
- Pre-existing heart and asthmatic conditions can also cause death when combined with ecstasy.

Paired
ACTIVITY

2 **Poster**

With your partner, design a poster warning teenagers about the effects of ecstasy on the body. Display the posters in your classroom.

5. Heroin

- Heroin is an opiate drug that was originally used to replace morphine as a painkiller.
- It has many other unofficial names such as smack, gear, horse.
- It is a white, odourless powder when pure.
- It turns darker and smells of vinegar as it gets older.
- Heroin users snort, smoke or inject the drug.
- Injecting drugs is referred to as taking drugs intravenously (IV).

Effects of heroin on the body

- Users describe the temporary feeling of euphoria as a 'rush'
- Pain suppression
- Nausea and vomiting, usually during the first encounter
- The body develops a tolerance quickly, so the user will need to use more on their next 'fix', every four or six hours

- Overdosing is common: users don't know how much of the heroin is pure, so they cannot tell exactly how much they are taking
- Respiratory failure leading to death
- Foetal death in pregnant women
- Hazy mental function
- Reduced sex drive
- Psychological dependence
- Depression
- Use of unhygienic needles can cause blood poisoning and infection of the heart valves
- The sharing of needles can transfer the HIV infection and hepatitis, which can cause damage to the liver
- Bronchitis due to respiratory failure

 Remember!

Heroin is extremely addictive and this addiction can develop very quickly.

1 Society

 What impact do you think heroin users have on society?

_____

_____

_____

2 Discussion

How would you know if you had an addiction to drugs?

What would be the signs?

Drug withdrawal

Withdrawal or 'cold turkey' is the term used when someone is trying to stop taking heroin. Withdrawal happens four to twelve hours after the last fix. The symptoms of withdrawal are:

- Tremors and headaches
- Sweating and goose pimples (hence the term 'cold turkey')
- Anxiety and irritability
- Nausea, vomiting, cramps and diarrhoea

6. Effects of drug use on society

Drug taking (remember this includes alcohol as well) has many effects on our communities.

1 **Impact on the community**

(a) With your partner, consider the following institutions/groups within your community and list two effects excessive drug use will have on them.

Group	Effect 1	Effect 2
Public transport	Antisocial behaviour – cursing, drinking etc.	People are afraid to use public transport
Hospitals		
Taxis		
Publicans		
Gardaí		
Shops		
Restaurants		
Schools		
Neighbours		
Pedestrians/cyclists		

(b) Identify three changes that could be made to remove or limit the impact of drug use on your community.

(i) _____

(ii) _____

(iii) _____

Impact of the drug industry on the environment

Rainforests in South and Central America are being cleared to grow coca plants. In the US, national forests are being destroyed to plant marijuana. Hazardous waste products from the manufacture of methamphetamines have a huge impact on safe water supply.

Knowing the facts about drugs

Some people think that taking drugs will relieve them of their problems, when in fact they bring even more problems.

Knowing the facts about drugs is essential; being fully aware of the risks involved will help you make the right decision. Make the decision **now** to say no to drugs; it will make it easier to continue to say no later on.

Help is available for those who have a drug problem. There are many organisations in Ireland to help young people give up their drug habit.

Helpful website:
Narcotics Anonymous Ireland –
www.na-ireland.org

End of Module Review

In small groups, write a short talk, poem or rap to deliver to First Years outlining the main reasons they should 'Say no to drugs'. One person from each group should then present this talk/poem/rap to the class.

_____

_____

_____

_____

_____

_____

_____

_____

_____

_____

_____

_____

_____

_____

_____

_____

_____

_____

Module 10

Personal Safety

This module examines the importance of being alert and aware of dangerous situations. We will also look at ways to protect yourself from threatening or abusive behaviour.

 Digital Resources are available for this module at mentorbooks.ie/resources

We will explore:

1. Responsibility for your personal safety

Personal safety is about taking responsibility to keep yourself safe from harm. Being aware of your surroundings and using a common sense approach to your own safety can reduce your chances of becoming a victim of crime. Being informed about various help agencies and the services they provide is also an important feature of a good personal safety plan.

Sometimes misunderstandings can occur between teenagers and adults as to who is responsible for teenagers' safety. This is probably because parents/guardians are used to protecting their children's personal safety, so letting go of that responsibility can be difficult for them. Teenagers can feel that they are capable of making decisions for themselves and that they are self-reliant when it comes to their own safety. The way to minimise the 'tug-of-war' effect would be for both sides to come up with an agreement about personal safety. This would involve both parties talking, listening and compromising.

1 **Disagreements**

Can you think of a recent situation where you argued with a parent/guardian over something that you wanted to do? Describe the situation under the following headings:

(a) What did you want to do at the time?

_____

_____

(b) Why might your parent/guardian have been angry or worried about this?

_____

_____

(c) Can you identify any risks that might be associated with this activity?

_____

_____

(d) What might you have said or done to stop your parent/guardian worrying about you?

_____

_____

Adults still play an important part in their teenage children's personal safety. This is because of their love and concern for them. Keeping adults informed about your everyday activities is not a sign of weakness; it shows those around you that you are mature and responsible enough to make your own decisions. It also keeps the channel of communication open for you to use in times of trouble.

2. Recognising unsafe situations

1 **Case studies**

Identify how the following characters have put themselves in potentially dangerous situations.

Case Study 1

Cilla often babysat for Mr and Mrs Browne. On one such occasion the phone rang thirty minutes after the Brownes had left. Cilla answered the phone, saying, 'Hello, Cilla speaking.' The caller was a man asking to speak with either Mr or Mrs Browne. Cilla answered, 'Oh, I'm sorry, you just missed them; they've gone out for the night.' The caller asked if there would be anyone in the house who could help him carry in a chest of drawers that he had promised to deliver. Cilla replied, 'I'm the only one here who can help, if it's not too heavy.'

Twenty minutes later the doorbell rang. Cilla opened the door. Outside was a man that Cilla had never seen before. He said, 'Hi, you must be Cilla, I'm Ralph. I was on the phone to you earlier about the chest of drawers. Would it be OK if I checked the size of the space for the chest before I bring it in?'

Cilla agreed and let him in.

(a) What could have happened to Cilla next?

_____

_____

(b) List five things Cilla did that she should **not** have done.

(i) _____

(ii) _____

(iii) _____

(iv) _____

(v) _____

Case Study 2

Howard's dad would not let him go to the teenage disco in the next town. He said it was too far away and that he'd heard that a lot of fights happened there afterwards.

Howard really wanted to go, so he told his dad that he was going to his friend Jason's house that night. Howard and Jason went to the disco. Howard had a fight with Jason and left the disco on his own.

Howard was unsure of the way back to the bus stop to get the 9 p.m. bus as planned. By the time he found the bus stop he had missed the bus.

He knew he would be in big trouble when he got home and thought that if he rang his dad and asked him to collect him he would be in worse trouble. No one else was waiting at the bus stop and it was getting dark.

While waiting for the next bus, which would be another hour, a car pulled up and the driver rolled down the window. The driver said, 'Hey, I know you, you live on the same road as me. Need a lift?' Howard recognised the driver. He was a little older than himself, and he did live on the same road and was always hanging around the estate at night laughing, shouting and annoying the neighbours. Howard had never spoken to him and didn't even know his name. He never knew he had a car either. Howard said, 'OK, thanks,' and got into the car.

(a) What could have happened to Howard next?

_____

_____

(b) List five things Howard should **not** have done.

(i) _____

(ii) _____

(iii) _____

(iv) _____

(v) _____

(c) What should Howard have done when the car pulled up at the bus stop?

_____

_____

Aware

Self-protection tips

Walking

1. Do not put all your necessities and valuables in the one bag; disperse your keys, phone and money into different pockets of your clothing. Carry your bag close to your body.

2. Walk on the kerb-side of the pavement rather than the inside of the path to avoid any bushes or alleyways where someone may be lurking.

3. Have the keys of the house in your hand to use in self-defence; this also means you don't have to fumble to find the keys when you get to your house.

4. If you think you are being followed, cross the road a few times to see if you are being copied. If you are still worried, go to the nearest place where there are people and call the Gardaí.

5. Always tell someone you trust where you are going in advance – this is just a precaution but may prove essential. It is also helpful in case someone needs to contact you.

6. Check that your mobile phone is fully charged and has enough credit in case you need to make future arrangements or ring in an emergency.

Public transport

1. Avoid waiting at isolated bus stops.

2. If the bus is empty, sit near the driver.

3. On a train, sit in a compartment where there are other people.

Taxis

1. Ensure you are travelling in a licensed taxi by checking the vehicle's plate and the driver's badge. Both should be clearly displayed.

2. When booking a taxi over the phone, ask for information concerning the vehicle as to its colour, make etc. Check it when it arrives.

3. Sit in the back seat if you are travelling alone.

4. If you feel uneasy, trust your instincts. Make an excuse to get out of the taxi at a safe, well-lit place where there are plenty of people.

WB3

2 **Staying alert**

Being 'street smart' is a common expression.

(a) What do you think it means?

_____

(b) List five ways in which a teenager can be street smart.

(i)   _____

(ii) _____

(iii) _____

(iv) _____

(v)   _____

(c) Using your five ideas above, draw an icon for each idea that would remind a teenager to stay safe. Note: you do not have to be great at drawing.

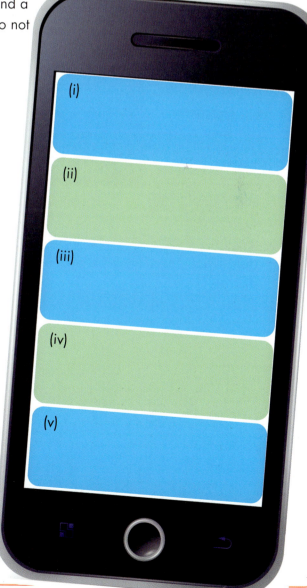

3. Violence

Violence is behaviour that can hurt or intimidate a person. Acts of violence can be psychological as well as physical.

1. **What is abuse?**

YOU DON'T NEED A BRUISE

TO BE ABUSED

Examine the image above. In small groups, discuss the following.

(a) What do you think the meanings are behind the logo?

(b) How does the logo makes you feel?

(c) Is the logo specific to gender, age, religion or culture?

NOTE
Culture means the ideas, traditions and behaviours of a particular people, e.g. the Irish.

Types of violence

Physical violence

- Physical attack
- Sexual assault

Psychological violence

- Emotional blackmail (this is an attack on the mentality of the victim. When someone in your life uses fear, guilt and/or a sense of duty to manipulate you.)
- Bullying
- Verbal abuse

2 **Psychological violence and verbal abuse**

Look at the poster below of a woman being harassed as she walks down the street and discuss the following questions with your partner.

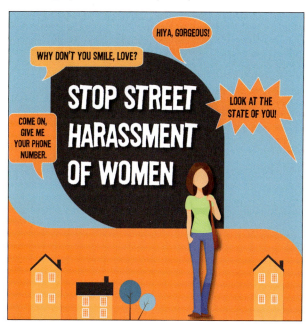

(a) How regularly do you think women experience suggestive name-calling as they go about their day-to-day lives?

(b) How do you think such suggestive name-calling could make a woman feel?

(c) Do men experience this too?

(d) What do you think a victim should do at the time? And what should they do after it has happened?

Such verbal abuse is a form of sexism. Other more dangerous forms of harassment can be groping, where a person touches or grabs another person in an inappropriate way. When such groping is sexually suggestive it is classed as a sexual assault, as it is sexually driven and done without the victim's consent.

NOTE
Sexism is when a person is discriminated against because of their gender.

TRB

3 Guys standing up against sexism

'At a fraternity house at a university in North Carolina, one of the most popular events to attract freshman pledges was to have girls from a sorority dress in bikinis and welcome guys to the house. This understandably attracted a lot of people. The guys would stare and talk about the girls. However, one year a fraternity brother hesitated and asked himself, "What if one of those girls was my sister?" He shared his mixed feelings with his fraternity brothers, and they decided to stop hosting the event.'

'The Importance of Respect in Teenage Sexuality', www.teenlife.com

NOTE
A **fraternity** is an organisation of male students; a **sorority** is an organisation of female students. **Freshman** pledges are new members.

The start of this story illustrates sexism. Can you find three pieces of evidence in the story to support this?

(a) _____

(b) _____

(c) _____

Healthy relationships need to be based on a foundation of respect. Battling gender inequality isn't about men versus women. It's about people against prejudice.

NOTE
Prejudice is an opinion that is not based on reason or actual experience.

4 Jogger fights back

I was jogging on my usual route when a car pulled up beside me. The driver opened his window and beckoned me over, saying, 'Excuse me, can you give me some directions?' I went over to the car and answered, 'If I can.' When I leaned into the window he grabbed my chest and started laughing while hurting me. I screamed while the two other male passengers laughed. I felt so angry and humiliated. Luckily I had my mobile phone with me and I managed to take a photograph of the car registration as they drove off. I later reported it to the Gardaí.

(a) Do you think what happened to the jogger was a sexual assault? Give a reason for your answer.

_____

_____

(b) After the assault, what actions did the jogger take to assert herself and her rights?

_____

_____

5 Case study

John is with his friends in the city at the skate park. He decides to leave early and walk home alone. Ahead there are other boys in hoodies, drinking cans, shouting aggressively and shoving each other. There is no-one else around.

What do you think he should do next?

_____

_____

Group
ACTIVITY

6 **Other types of harassment**

In small groups, discuss the following.

(a) Are there any particular groups that you think might suffer from public harassment?

(b) What actions do you think could be taken to prevent this bullying behaviour?

NOTE
If you are concerned or upset about any of the issues we have discussed in this section, speak to your teacher or one good adult: they will help you.

4. Safety on the Internet

The Internet is a great tool for school projects, education, chatting with friends, games and much more. It provides knowledge and information on a vast amount of subjects, so much so that it must be used with caution. Most teenagers are familiar with computers: how they operate, how to use search engines and how to get on to various sites. Many parents are concerned about the type of material their children can access and the type of people who can access their child through the Internet. It is therefore important for parents and teenagers to establish guidelines for Internet use to minimise the risks involved.

NOTE
See also *Module 3: Communication Skills* in both *Minding Me 1: My Well-Being* and *Minding Me 2: My Well-Being*.

Internet use rules

1. Keep personal information private. Do not send a photo of yourself, reveal your real name, your e-mail address, home address, your mobile number or family information.

2. Never reply to any hostile or suggestive e-mails. Inform your parents and your Internet Service Provider of such e-mails.

3. Do not fill out surveys or contests that request your e-mail address or you may find your inbox will be full of spam on next checking. These sites send or sell your e-mail address to other sites! Predators can gain access in this way.

4. Do not believe a stranger is who they say they are, even if they send you a picture. It is easy to pretend you are someone else on the Internet.

5. Do not arrange to meet anyone you have communicated with through the Internet unless your parents are with you.

6. Do not believe that you will get 'something for nothing' by entering competitions. These sites are trying to sell you something and want to find out more about you to sell you more things!

7. Think seriously before you post any personal information to social networking sites like Twitter, Facebook or Instagram. Once you send it into cyberspace it is out there forever for all to see.

8. Do not contribute to any 'hate literature'. Hate literature is when a person or a group is targeted because of their race, religion or beliefs. This is also a form of bullying.

9. Protect your computer from viruses and spam. Free antivirus software is available from AVG, Avast and many other companies.

① **Safety**

Can you think of any other way to stay safe when using the Internet?

_____

Helpful website:
www.thinkuknow.co.uk
www.safeteens.com
www.kidshealth.org/teen/safety
www.getsafeonline.org

The Internet never forgets

Paris Brown, the UK's first Youth Police and Crime Commissioner, had to resign her post at age 17, following criticism of messages she had posted on Twitter which could be considered racist and homophobic. She posted these offensive comments between the ages of 14 and 16.

ACTIVITY

2 **Lessons learned**

Learn more about her story at bbc.com – search for 'Paris Brown'.

List two things you have learned from what happened to her.

(a) _____

(b) _____

5. Mobile phone safety

CSPE

Mobile Phone Safety Rules

1. Only give your mobile phone number to people you know well and can trust.

2. Never reply to text messages from people you don't know.

3. Make sure you know how to block others from calling your phone. You should check this with your network provider.

4. If you have Bluetooth technology on your phone, you will be able to communicate with other Bluetooth-enabled phones in the vicinity. You may receive unwanted messages from other Bluetooth phone users, who may be able to access information stored on your phone (for example, someone could copy your contact list). You could consider switching off Bluetooth to prevent this.

5. Think about how a text message might be read before you send it. Just like e-mail, text messages can be taken the wrong way. Sending someone a text that could be misunderstood might upset them.

6. You should never give anyone else's number out without asking them if it is OK first, because you never know what it's going to be used for. If the person asking is genuine, they will not mind you saying 'No' until you have checked that it is OK.

7. You should never take pictures of anyone with your phone without their permission. Some people simply do not like having their photograph taken, so it would be better to ask them first.

8. Be careful if you meet someone in real life whom you only 'know' through text messaging. Even though text messaging is often the 'next step' after online chatting, that does not mean that it is safer. You do not really know with whom you are talking/texting and they might not be telling you the truth about themselves. With any face-to-face meeting, you should tell someone where you are going, take someone with you and arrange to meet in daylight in a public place (e.g. your local shopping centre).

9. Don't be a target. Wandering around with your phone in plain view can be dangerous. If you are not using it, put it in your pocket or your bag and only use it in public when absolutely necessary.

10. If you receive a nasty or bullying text, keep the message and show it to your one good adult. Make a note of the date and time of such messages or calls you receive.

TRB

Distracted-walking is a safety concern

Accident and Emergency visits have increased greatly because of the amount of pedestrians not paying attention to their own personal safety due to being distracted by their phones. Talking on phones, texting or listening to music has led to serious injuries and in some cases even death.

We need to rethink our relationship with our mobile phones and how distracted-walking while using such a device can have a serious impact on our lives.

NOTE
Holding a mobile phone while driving a mechanically propelled vehicle (e.g. a car) incurs three to five penalty points on a driver's licence and a maximum fine of €90.

1 Distracted-walking checklist

Are you putting your safety at risk? Tick the boxes that apply to you.

While walking do you:

	Yes	No
• Read and send texts?	☐	☐
• Use headphones?	☐	☐
• Have phone conversations?	☐	☐
• Think you have checked the traffic as you chat?	☐	☐
• Cross the road while you talk on the phone?	☐	☐

Even if you ticked only one box you are at risk. On average four pedestrians per day sustain an injury from distracted-walking while using a mobile phone, talking on the phone being the most common activity at the time of injury.

2 Did you know?

Wireless devices are the number-one pedestrian distraction, causing two types of distraction:

- **Visual:** eyes off where you are walking
- **Cognitive:** mind off where you are going

Which do you think is more distracting – eyes off or mind off?

Answer: They are both risky behaviour and equally distracting to the pedestrian.

5. Help agencies

From the topics we have investigated over the last three years, you will notice how sometimes we can't solve our own problems or difficulties and we need some outside help and advice. Help from our families and friends can be really positive, but sometimes your difficulty might be with a family member or friend and you will need an outsider's opinion or help.

The advice given in most agencies will be confidential; they will respect your feelings and try to offer help.

How to contact an agency

WB1

When deciding to contact an agency, it might be a good idea to write down what you want to say before you call the number.

Where can I get these contact addresses or telephone numbers?

A number of options are available:
- In school your guidance counsellor will have access to this information.
- Some agencies are listed below.
- You can look up agencies online.

What happens when I ring an agency?

- All agencies will work differently, but you will probably get to speak to a trained counsellor who will listen to what you have to say.
- Remember that anything you say is confidential and anonymous (if you want it to be).
- The counsellor may ask you some questions, but remember you can decide not to answer (assertive communication); the person will have your best interests at heart and will offer you advice and suggest ways to talk to family members or friends.

Support services for young people

CHILDLINE
Twenty-four-hour support and information service for children and teenagers
Phone: 1800 666 666
Teentext: Text TALK to 50101.
Text BULLY to 50101.
www.childline.ie

Suicide Aware
Twenty-four-hour support for those who are feeling suicidal or have been bereaved by suicide.
Helpline: 1800 742 745

Samaritans
Twenty-four-hour confidential support service for anyone who is in crisis.
Helpline: 1850 60 90 90
www.samaritans.org

TeenLine
Support helpline for teenagers.
Helpline: 1800 833 634
Free text TEEN to 50015
www.teenline.ie

SpunOut
An interactive website for young people which deals with a wide variety of issues.
www.spunout.ie

ISPCC
Irish Society for the Prevention of Cruelty to Children
Phone: 01 676 7960
www.ispcc.ie

ReachOut
An online youth mental-health service, helping you get through tough times.
ie.reachout.com

Remember!

You are not alone.

Practising sensible ways to protect yourself will ensure that you are not taking your personal safety for granted. Being aware of safety procedures provides you with the skills for self-protection – skills, hopefully, that you will never have to use.

End of Module Review

Compile a list of strategies that teenagers can use to keep themselves and their possessions safe when they are out and about. Discuss the ideas in class and write down those that everyone agrees are the best. Use the ideas to design a safety quiz, which could then be used to promote safety on the streets to other classes in your school.

NOTE
The safety quiz could also feature in your school's student magazine or website.

Reflection/End of Year Review

Start as you mean to go on

The activities presented in this book were designed to get every class member active in contributing towards establishing a sense of trust, understanding, equality and respect. Activities encouraged everyone to:

- **Take time** to think and share how their values, beliefs and behaviour impact on their own and others' health and well-being

- **Branch out** from their routine to make new friends, find like-minded people and develop skills for making personal and group decisions, while respecting their own dignity and the dignity of others

- **Enjoy** the natural diversity of their class and school community and look for friends and viewpoints from all walks of life

> *Never lose sight of the fact that the most important yardstick of your success will be how you treat other people – your family, friends, and co-workers, and even strangers you meet along the way.*
>
> Barbara Bush

ACTIVITY

1 **Reflection**

In the brick spaces below write in some of the parts of SPHE you have enjoyed and that you feel have helped you become the person you are today.

SCAFFOLDING

BY
SEAMUS HEANEY

Masons, when they start upon a building,
Are careful to test out the scaffolding;

Make sure that planks won't slip at busy points,
Secure all ladders, tighten bolted joints.

And yet all this comes down when the job's done
Showing off walls of sure and solid stone.

So if, my dear, there sometimes seem to be
Old bridges breaking between you and me

Never fear. We may let the scaffolds fall
Confident that we have built our wall.

END OF YEAR HEALTH REVIEW

Day	Exercise		Rest		Eating			
	Activity	Time spent	Sleep	Rest	Breakfast	Lunch	Dinner	No. of snacks
Monday (example)	Walked to school	20 min	8 hours	1 hour TV	Cereal, toast, juice	Sandwich, apple, fruit juice	Spaghetti bolognese	3
Monday								
Tuesday								
Wednesday								
Thursday								
Friday								
Saturday								
Sunday								

Notes

Notes

Notes

Notes

Notes